Advan.

'Dr. Meghan Walker is a true visionary, offering viable solutions for busy practitioners looking for more impact while becoming aligned and profitable. If you are looking to have more impact, legendary leadership, and to practice efficiency, then this book is for you. One of the best investments I made for my business was aligning myself with Meghan and her brilliance'.

—**Dr. Michelle Peris**, ND, creator of the Wild Collective

'If you are a medical practitioner, you probably feel like you could be doing more. You may feel frustrated with the economics of healthcare and the fact that you can only help so many patients in a day. IMPACT Medicine by Dr. Meghan Walker may be your pathway to greater fulfilment. Dr. Walker can help you to reach more people through books, online content, and social media. I've personally seen her achieve this in her own life and help others as well'.

—**Alan Christianson**, NMD, board-certified naturopathic endocrinologist and *New York Times* bestselling author of *The Thyroid Reset Diet*

'Meghan is the innovator and disrupter that medicine has been desperate for. Our system of burnt-out practitioners and uninspired patients has been landlocked in a broken model of one-to-one care and patchwork health. IMPACT is the system we need and the inspiration we crave'.

—**Dr. Jordan Robertson**, ND, CEO of the Confident Clinician and Clarity Health Network

'Healthcare is in desperate need of bold new leadership to solve some of our most complex challenges. Dr. Meghan Walker is one such leader, leaving a legacy of empowerment in all she touches. This book can open the door for you'.

—**James Maskell**, CEO and Founder of HealCommunity

'Dr. Meghan Walker and IMPACT Medicine provide a unique insight into the many ways a practitioner's business itself can change the lives of their patients. This book is a must-have manual for any practitioner looking to make a massive impact with their work'.

—**J. J. Virgin**, four-time *New York Times* bestselling author, celebrity nutritionist, and Founder of the Mindshare Collaborative

'This is the playbook every [clinician entrepreneur, health practitioner, health professional, doctor, healer] NEEDS. Step by step, Meghan shares what matters most to craft a [fulfiling, meaningful, impactful, rewarding] practice that builds lasting health for people'.

—**Ulrich Iserloh**, Founder of Big Boost Marketing Group

IMPACT
MEDICINE

TAKE CONTROL OF YOUR PRACTICE.
REACH MORE PEOPLE.
ADD BALANCE TO YOUR LIFE.

MEGHAN WALKER

LIONCREST
PUBLISHING

Impact Medicine

Take Control of Your Practice. Reach More People. Add Balance to Your Life.

ISBN 978-1-5445-3713-9 Hardcover

978-1-5445-3714-6 Paperback

978-1-5445-3715-3 Ebook

*To my adoring family and
the families who will be impacted by the
practitioners who read this book—
this is all for you.*

CONTENTS

PART THREE: **P OF PATIENTS (THE PEOPLE YOU SERVE)**

PART FOUR: **ATTRACTION**

INTRODUCTION

'How was your doctor's appointment? Any insight'?

'Alright. She said I am fine'.

And so, it begins. The awkward journey along the 'Line of Fine'. The precarious balancing act between symptoms that suggest health is compromised and bloodwork that doesn't capture anything except disease.

The Line of Fine is a place. It is a destination. It is the journey's end for the interactions and interventions that characterize our modern relationship with medicine. When patients reach the Line of Fine, they free up a bed, vacate a waiting room and enable the overwhelmed clinician to move on to the next patient on their list.

Reaching the Line of Fine does not mean that someone has achieved health; it means that they have achieved stabilization, symptom management or a phase of watchful waiting. It is a dangerous place for us to stop as a society. It leaves our systems, practitioners and citizens on edge, literally.

The way we manage disease is not the same as how we build health. And being fine does not mean that health has been achieved. For practitioners like you, like me and the countless others committed to moving people past the Line of Fine, we recognize the limitations and the role of the traditional system, but we want something more. We want to help people address the cause of their illness; we want to help them approach watchful waiting from a stance or proactivity. We want people dying happy in their old age, not young from chronic, preventable disease. The tools and credentials we carry to achieve these outcomes are plentiful and effective. Collectively, we cannot only change the course of health for our patients, but I would venture to say, society at-large.

And yet, we are deeply challenged in executing on our own potential. We are facing a challenge. Despite the tools in our toolbox, the efficacy of our interventions and the clear potential of our respective modalities to transform the lives of the people we serve, we struggle.

Our challenge, at its core, is that the model, systems, businesses and offerings required to get people to 'fine' are not the same that we require to get people to true health.

This book is the roadmap for clinicians who want to pick people up at the Line of Fine. This book is the roadmap for clinicians who want more impact and greater insight into designing a business that in and of itself contributes to the delivery of health. This book is for those who understand that the definition of 'insanity' is taking the same action but expecting different results. This book defines a new course of action.

Pairing symptoms with a disease title and treatment is a hallmark feature of the pathogenic model of care—the 'fixing side' of the Line of Fine—and it isn't working. Rather than digging deeper to learn the patient's habits and behaviours that might be creating the health issue, the pathogenic provider's typical response is to offer a temporary solution, most conveniently packaged as pharmaceutical. It's the fastest recourse in a system desperate to get people to the finish line.

When we solve symptoms alone with a drug, we're not getting to the root of what's going on. We're simply alleviating the physiological noise *for both providers and patients*. Whether we do this because of our training or because it appears to be the most efficient way to treat someone is irrelevant—what does matter is that there is another way for you, and for your patients. This other way not only has the capacity to address the root cause of the problem, but it can additionally support your practice financially *and* enable broad patient access to deeper healing opportunities.

The model that builds health on the opposite side of the Line of Fine is called IMPACT Medicine.

Exploring this model does not mean I am pointing a finger at you specifically or at any of our fellow colleagues. We're all simply working under the assumption that our formal training taught us everything we need to know to get people on the road to health. But I don't believe that is the case. There's one critical, underlying concept that has been absent in all of our training, and that is the *business* education and entrepreneurial thinking necessary to run a successful practice that works better for you and for the people you serve. This part of the model is what makes our care accessible. That's right—the answers to the chronic disease epidemic lie in entrepreneurial thinking. Not in the realm of startups and technology, but through the system-driven lens that entrepreneurial problem-solving can facilitate. I'll tell you how and why entrepreneurial thinking solves the healthcare problem, but first, let's look at the current state of global health and why the world needs us to heed this message and model now more than ever.

A TIPPING POINT

You and I never wanted to simply alleviate problems. We didn't spend all that time, effort and expense attending medical school or post-graduate training to simply mitigate symptoms—most of us wanted to truly help people heal. Think of it this way: If we came across people floating down a river, panicked and drowning, as helpers, we would pull them ashore, one after the other, and assist in their rescue. This would be an endless role so long as people kept coming. But we would it. Eventually, or perhaps alternatively, we could paddle our boat upstream to find out why they were falling into the river in the first place. Practitioners like us don't want to rely on a resuscitation model of patient management—we want to go further upstream to find a solution that's deeper than symptomatic control.

If we want to find answers to the lingering issues in our industry, however, something needs to change. This is especially true today, on the backside of a pandemic, and in a political landscape desperate for solutions that increase the capacity of our healthcare systems.

In 2020, Western society's health was at a tipping point. An epidemic of chronic disease built on decades of unhealthy eating habits, sleep habits, and stressful lifestyles had pushed the health of many people to the edge of a precipice from which recovery seemed unlikely, if not impossible. The incidence of cardiovascular disease had increased by double-digits over the prior two decades. Nearly three-quarters of adults in the US alone were overweight or obese. For the first time in history, children born in that country had a shorter life expectancy than their parents. Along with physical health issues, mental illness around the world was also on the rise. A significant increase in psychological disorders, particularly among young adults, marked the years leading up to 2020. We were deeply immersed in an epidemic of poor health. We were sitting ducks.

When the coronavirus pandemic hit, the tipping point was sharpened, and millions of people were pushed over the edge. The medical community responded the way it always had: by managing the acute manifestations and systemic weaknesses exposed by decades of festering chronic disease. Like dry arid grassland, the epidemic of chronic disease left our society and healthcare systems exposed and vulnerable to the influence of lightning or a stray cigarette or a rogue virus. While the traditional approach to healthcare was an appropriate short-term response to a worldwide disaster, it fell horribly short in regard to treating the ongoing chronic disease epidemic that had been growing for a generation, and which continues to plague the lives of people across the Western world.

That epidemic requires a new approach—one that asks the right questions and prioritizes the patient over the disease, seeking answers to why and how a person develops a condition, treating the causes along with the symptoms, relieving or eliminating the source and preempting further illness.

SICK AND TIRED OF IT ALL

If you're a practitioner, I'm not telling you anything you don't already know. You want to help people—that's why you got into this business in the first place. You're not likely happy with the state of healthcare or your practice, but you're struggling to find a solution. The current model of one-to-one patient care is time-intensive but seems necessary. It's all we know. It's what our mentors and our colleagues do. Yet, we can't seem to get any traction in this ongoing chronic disease epidemic. Some days, we question whether we're even making a difference.

While we're concerned for the health outcomes of our patients, we're not exactly thrilled with our own situations either. The hours are long, and the pay isn't what we expected—not for the amount of time we put in. Just running a practice eats up every hour of our day and every dime in our pocket. There are university loans, employees' salaries, and insurance to pay. It seems the only people who can afford to practice are the independently wealthy or those with a spouse with a good-paying job to support them. Since when did being a practitioner become the domain of the elite?

Humans are meant to evolve. We adapt to our surroundings, and over time, what's normal one day is out of date the next. New tools are needed and developed to complete any given job, creating a new process that will, itself, change over time. Yet, somehow, the healthcare industry doesn't seem to operate in the same manner. In healthcare, we continue to use the same tools in every situation. No matter the patient or their scenario, the mindset seems to stay the same: *temporary relief. Just get them to fine!* We aren't innovating or improving health, just how we patch the holes. This approach is failing everyone.

There are lots of obstacles to making change: Political will and the time needed to test and implement new hypotheses simply isn't there. Rates of clinician burnout are soaring throughout every speciality, and with a growing population and further need to treat more and more patients, little time remains for the adoption of new practices. If we keep up at this pace, though, our industry and the people we serve are in big trouble. We can see the danger ahead.

THE ROAD TO RECOVERY

In 1908, the Ford Motor Company introduced the Model T. It was the first financially accessible vehicle that laid the groundwork for the modern car-obsessed culture of the United States. In 1916, the US government first funded an attempt to build a national road grid, and in 1956, Dwight D. Eisenhower introduced legislation that would lead to the creation of a complete national highway system. This system was finally proclaimed completed in 1992 at a cost equivalent to $535 billion. The car, bus and truck had no choice but to remain a fixture in American transportation. So much had been invested in their integration into modern American life that few innovations had the room or financial incentivization to succeed. As the old saying goes, 'When the only tool you carry is a hammer, everything is a nail'.

Healthcare delivery is like the US highway system. We are so heavily invested in the infrastructure, schooling, support industries and micro-economies that there are few incentives to think of, fund or deploy solutions and approaches that fall outside the box of traditional thinking. In healthcare, we have become so zoned into a singular way of doing things—of investing all of our resources into building those roads, bridges and durable cars—that we try to leverage the system (and our societal investment) for every situation. But you can't build health with the same system that fixes disease. They require different vehicles. In the end, this strategy causes burnout for clinicians and a deeper separation between healthcare workers and patients.

Want proof? Just take a look at how many patients are seeking methods of self-diagnosis and self-treatment through the internet today. People are looking for opportunities to take control of their health. Not simply because they lack trust in the healthcare system (which, I believe, is falling rapidly), it's their lack of patience for the revolving door process currently being implemented. Health consumers don't want to view their healthcare as a transaction; they want a transformation, or to see some continuous, positive results. As clinicians, we want this too. What would it take for our goals to align?

The first challenge is our reliance on a transactional approach to care—the one that's been around forever and that we have been taught to replicate. It perfectly serves the need of triage and patch medicine, but transactions are poorly suited to drive transformational change. And if that wasn't a big enough problem, as we try to see more patients and complete more transactions, we lose focus on our own health—and wealth—in the process. Basically, we're using the wrong tools for the job. We're trying to drive that car over water to meet up with our friend, and we're getting frustrated when the car sinks.

Think about your current role and relationship with patients. Everything you do for them is provided on a one-to-one level, consuming your time and theirs, while doing little to move the needle of their overall health forward. Is it any surprise that so many of us are suffering from burnout?

For practitioners aiming to address the root cause of disease, the pathogenic, transactional approach to healthcare is detrimental to your finances, not to mention your patients' wallets. You're constantly trading time for money, and the inefficiency of the model drives up the cost (and financial risk) of this model of care.

For patients seeking care on the opposite side of the Line of Fine, the entire infrastructure of the medical field needs to change. From hospitals to doctors' offices and medical literature and training to our delivery and care models—it all needs to acknowledge the difference between fixing and building health. We need to park the car in the garage and move away from the transactional, pathogenic model of care.

ENTER IMPACT MEDICINE

IMPACT Medicine is a transformational approach to healthcare and the business of health delivery. It picks up at the Line of Fine. It's a model that *promotes health building* over alleviating symptoms or managing disease. The goal at the end of the day should be for us to see our patients *less*—to provide them with the education and a plan necessary for their health to thrive, so they don't require regular Band-Aid visits for new prescriptions and short-term remedies. They need empowerment over their own health and a guide to show them the way. They need a transformational approach to building their own state of health.

What does that do for us, as practitioners? For one, it opens up time in our schedules, so we aren't dedicating every waking moment to one-to-one patient care. Transformation is not only possible with tools and models beyond one-to-one care, it is necessary. Many clinicians go straight from university to practicing and get so caught up in the whirlwind of patient care, they put off other goals in their life, like starting a family or pursuing personal interests. Our own health goals suffer. There isn't time to go to the gym, make a salad or train for a marathon when you're seeing patients from nine to five every day and doing paperwork all evening. We have created a model of practicing healthcare that requires a clinician to be available all the time, at the expense of their own happiness and, ironically, health.

Transforming to a new way of treating patients can promote better health for both you and your patients. I don't know about you, but this concept appeals to my 'cake and eat it too' personality. With all that you've sacrificed so far, why shouldn't you ask for the moon for yourself as well as your patients? For your patients, it not only removes them from the transactional 'revolving door' and enables them to lead healthier, happier lives. You, the clinician, get the luxury of more time for a life outside of work. No more long hours, late nights, and frantic emails supporting patients who seem to require constant care. You don't need to be living that life, and trust me, most of your patients don't want that life either.

The IMPACT Medicine solution involves a two-fold approach: (1) Recognize the opportunity in reaching patients beyond simply one-to-one care through a new proactive model of care; and (2) Address the unique needs of building health on the opposite side of the Line of Fine. Rather than the pathogenic, transactional approach to patient care, the opportunity before us allows for an adoption of a 'biopsychosocial-informed model' for caring for patients. The biopsychosocial-informed model considers the intersection and interaction between the biological, social and psychological factors that inform health.

The biopsychosocial model of care was first developed in 1977 by George Engel and Don Romano. The model acknowledges the interplay between biology, psychology and sociological factors in the development and, ultimately, the resolution of illness. It is contrasted with the biologic/pathogenic model that drives most health policy and interventional care models.

A biopsychosocial approach to care, mixed with the entrepreneurial strategies I have implemented from my own experience as a clinician entrepreneur, has allowed me to guide hundreds of practitioners to a rejuvenated, accelerated practice that benefits them financially, emotionally and physically, helping them provide better care while enjoying more time for their personal lives.

THE STORY BEHIND IT ALL

Before becoming a Naturopathic Doctor, I was an entrepreneur. As a seventeen-year-old high school student, I started a cottage-cleaning business and grew my team, so I could spend my summers on the dock. Even then, I knew that starting and running businesses was my passion. Around the same time, I experienced some health challenges that brought me to a Naturopathic Doctor. Inspired by that experience and struck by the intelligence of his questioning, I couldn't shake my interest in approaching medicine and health from this perspective. I sold my business and entered university, focussing first on biological sciences and then went on to study Naturopathic Medicine.

For a while, my entrepreneurial spirit took a back seat to my medical career. I graduated from naturopathic medical school, co-founded a practice and began running the Integrated Health Institute with a friend and fellow Naturopathic Doctor, Erin Wiley. The clinic was successful, but the workload combined with the day-to-day activity of seeing patients wore on me, and burnout soon kicked in. Almost any doctor you speak with today can relate to this, and my circumstances were no different. Some days, I was spending too many hours seeing too many patients, with no time for myself—not even to take care of my own health. Other days, we were hustling to drive new traffic through the door. Erin and I were endlessly trying to innovate efficiencies within the clinic, but with every passing year, even as we were doing great things, I felt as if I was getting further behind on my vision for contribution. I had to get clear on what I wanted for my life and career. One thing was abundantly clear: running the clinic and being part of a practice where I saw patients on a daily basis wasn't the exact path for me. Clarity around my personal mission was emerging at an unstoppable speed; I wanted to put this preventative system of medicine into the hands of millions of people. This could not happen in my clinical practice alone. It would need to happen by galvanizing and supporting the work of my colleagues and those equally committed to practicing preventative care. This was the moment where I became more committed to my mission than the model in which it manifested.

I stepped away from the clinic, on good terms, and I also sold my share in the practice. A concept was beginning to form in my mind, a business strategy in the healthcare system that put what I referred to as 'upstream medicine' in the hands of practitioners and patients. Around the same time, I was offered a CEO position at a startup company that connected consumers to healthcare practitioners and providers. While leading this new startup (and breastfeeding my second child, my six-week-old daughter), I adjacently ran my own 'micro-practice' so that I could continue to work with my patients. My goal with this new model of practice was to work half the time and double my income. Cake and eat it too, right?

From there, my mission expanded. I became obsessed with health, high performance and entrepreneurship, and I was in search of a way to integrate all of these things, so I could deliver healthcare that worked for me and for my patients. I wanted more time (cue two kids under three) and more money (cue two kids under three), but most of all, I wanted more impact from the time I spent away from my small kids. When I started to get more mail per day from the listeners to my podcast than I got per year from my patients, I knew there was a new model I could deploy. A model where I could still inspire health, while moving my mission of putting 'upstream/

root-cause' medicine in the hands of thirty million people by 2030. I was clear; I was more committed to my mission than the model in which it developed.

There was still so much to figure out, beginning with how best to leverage all that I'd learned at school. How could we, as clinicians, put this incredibly powerful system of healing—addressing the root cause of the problem instead of just dealing with the symptoms—into the hands of more people? How could we overcome obstacles to this goal, such as the lack of efficiency and sustainability in traditional practitioners' businesses?

Sure, while each day I was becoming more clear and living on purpose, I was still wearing too many hats. I was working too much and not making the kind of impact—or income—I believed was possible.

One day, as I was in the checkout line in the grocery store, I looked up at the flashing $30 million–lottery drawing and asked myself a familiar question:

What would be different tomorrow if I won?

Until that day, my answer was always the same: *nothing*. That day, however, a different answer came streaming out of my subconscious:

I'd stop seeing patients.

I had left the Integrated Health Institute and my first practice with a goal of creating a new practice that allowed me to have the life I wanted, and I also wanted to satisfy this goal of supporting and improving the lives of practitioners and their patients. That was a lot, and there was no way to squeeze in seeing patients on a one-to-one basis. I had reached a point where I couldn't simultaneously be present with patients and pushing towards these bigger goals. I was becoming burnt out, risking my own health while spending all of my time trying to improve the health of others. It made no sense. Something had to give, and I made the decision to be ruthlessly focused on creating the impact I wanted while supporting practitioners in the creation of their ideal lives as well.

I didn't win the lottery, but seeing those numbers did instil something in me that stuck. That initial thought—*I'd stop seeing patients*—made me think long and hard about where my career was going, and the next day, I decided to take a sabbatical from patient care.

Being away from the office gave me time to reflect. It allowed me the mental capacity to think about things other than patient care, and in that short time, my eyes were opened to the downfalls of the current system—that transactional model of care delivery. I discovered, during this time off, that something needed to change, not only with the way we providers operate our practices but also in how we view patient healthcare.

I also knew that I wanted to make a bigger impact on the world. I knew I wanted to help people, but what I was currently doing didn't seem to be helping enough. I wanted to be contributing on a larger scale and making a more significant impact. I wanted to reach my own version of thirty million.

In that moment, in front of that sign, I took a leap. I made the choice to leave patient care to help define a new model of practice. I returned from the store and immediately reached out to my team.

My sabbatical started eight weeks later. And I never returned to practice. I have also never looked back.

LET THIS BE YOUR ROADMAP

Are you ready for me to show you the roadmap that will allow you to think clearer, provide stronger patient outcomes and attract more people towards health? Good! Because I'm ready to share it with you.

This isn't a rule book on how to build better health or a better practice. It's a *framework* for doing so. It's a map that will guide you towards a new way of health—and wealth—building.

It's permission for you to start saying, 'Yes, *and'*, not 'Yes, *but'*. Yes, you can still continue seeing patients and helping people. *And* you can also have more satisfaction from your role as a healthcare practitioner, have the financial freedom you expected when you chose this career, have more time to live the life you thought you'd have by now and—believe it or not—help even more people than you ever thought possible.

It's the path to making an IMPACT as a practitioner and, yes, an entrepreneur. The parts are simple, and there are just six:

- ▶ Part One: **I**ntention—Know what you want and why you want it.
- ▶ Part Two: **M**indset—Get your head in the game, and play like a winner.
- ▶ Part Three: **P** of Patients (the People You Serve)— You can't save the world, but you can be selective about

serving the people who can benefit the most from what you have to offer.

- ► Part Four: **A**ttraction—This is not the field of dreams. After you build your model, you need to bring the right people through the door.
- ► Part Five: **C**ents and Sense—Helping others and financial freedom are not mutually exclusive. You really can have your cake and eat it too.
- ► Part Six: **T**hinking Like an Entrepreneur—By this point, you'll be on your way, but there's more.

These six parts have worked for me and for the many practitioners who've followed this framework. In my mission to help even more people, I know the steps outlined in this book will help you and your patients too.

Are you ready to start getting granular in your goals of helping others? Ready to make your own IMPACT while also securing a financial legacy for you and your family? Then, let's get clear on your purpose and your goals. Let's get clear on *Part One*: your **I**ntention.

PART ONE

INTENTION

'When your intention is clear, so is the way'.

—Alan Cohen

have a slide inside my house. The icy blue tube slide runs right through my main hallway and into the playroom below. This slide wasn't in our home when we bought it. This was not the leftover decision of the odd owners who lived there before... this was 100 per cent a reflection of my own vision and intention for fun and play in my home.

Intention is the 'I' in IMPACT Medicine, and it's where we begin. Intention requires clarity around what you want. Unfortunately, many people never get this clarity, and they wind up in situations that don't fulfil their true desires. Often, they settle for a life and a career that deprives them of their full potential, happiness and financial freedom. How do people get into these situations? Well, not intentionally, that's for sure. They land there by happenstance, floating like a stick in a river instead of navigating in a boat. They make decisions about their lives and careers based on what they thought they wanted, what everyone else was doing or what others wanted for them. Too often, people make the safe or easy decision in the moment without considering the consequences or their true desires.

This is not a challenge unique to clinicians, but the consequences for us are often more damaging. With high levels of student loans and delayed earning potential in our careers, there is less wiggle room for poorly crafted life plans. The typical practitioner pursues a healthcare profession because they want to help people. Many will tell you that helping others is a calling. Yet, joining the industry places them in a physically and emotionally demanding position that tests their own happiness and, by extension, their fulfilment. For many, the degree was the end goal and intentionality beyond that point was never a consideration or a project to be tackled later.

And it's not as if practitioners aren't aware of the strain. Most know they want something to change, but they don't have the time, capacity or the bandwidth to figure it out. They need clarity around where they are now and where they would like to be, so they can be intentional about their choices going forward.

Someday, they think they'll figure it out, they say... Someday, when the work slows down. Someday, when they aren't so busy. The problem is that the work will never slow down. In fact, their practices are busier than ever. And the demands on their time are ever-increasing.

Healthcare professionals have little time to strategize in domains they don't understand or to which they haven't been previously exposed. They can't spare even a day to take a step back and look at how they're running their practices. Even if the time could be found, there isn't a roadmap to follow or a broader system with an appetite for change. *If only the model existed*, they say, then they would certainly be providing better care to more people without working so hard to make that happen. And they'd have happier, more fulfilled lives themselves.

It's not surprising that so many of us are in this situation. We're lifelong students who have become very adept at following directions. All those years of schooling taught us to follow the rules to be successful. We dread failure, especially considering the dire outcomes of medical failure, so we stick to the tried and true, never considering the 'what ifs'. We never think about what it might be like to put a big blue slide in our living room.

I started out the same way. And it wasn't until I gained ruthless clarity about what I wanted my life and career to look like, and became *intentional* about getting it, that I was brave enough to leave that old life and career behind. I knew there had to be a better way, and I figured it out. I stepped out of the shadows of 'in the box' thinking and into the light of innovation around how I delivered services. For me, there was no looking back. And it all started with clarity of intention.

CHAPTER 1

LIVING FOR IMPACT

When we started looking seriously for a home, I thought about what I needed. My husband and I were living in a small rental home with our first child, and I was pregnant with our second. We needed more space for our growing family, but that desire was only the beginning.

Our real estate agent asked, 'What do you want? What's your ideal home?'

I don't think my agent was prepared for my answer. My ideal home would be on a specific street in Toronto, Walker Avenue. It was a lovely street but was, as importantly, named after my family dating back to when my great-great-great-grandparents had a carriage factory on the corner. In addition to location, we wanted a home with a suite where my mother-in-law could live, with her own entrance and kitchen, and not in the basement. Her apartment would need to be on the second floor where she'd have windows and a lot of light. And the requests didn't end there...

To afford a place like we were describing, we'd need it to also have the capacity to provide a rental property income, so the house would require at least a third unit that we could rent. Could a home like that possibly exist? I didn't know, but I wasn't going to limit my vision.

Miraculously—and I mean *miraculously*—our real estate agent said she knew just the house for us. The catch was that it wasn't on the market, but he reached out to the homeowners, and they agreed to let us see the place. We toured the house. It needed work, but it checked *all* of the boxes. We could only afford to pay fair market value—a rare occurrence in the heated Toronto real estate market. Would they be willing to sell?

We did the deal.

Eventually, we got to a point where we could afford the mortgage without the rental unit, so we reclaimed those rooms and had the place renovated. Again, instead of going down the traditional path, I thought about what was possible. That's when I remembered the tube slide.

When I was a kid, I had asked my father (as one does) for a giant tube slide inside our home. Naturally, he said no, but added that if I still wanted a slide in my home when I was an adult, I would have the privilege of putting it there myself. Here was my chance to finally get what I really wanted, and not in the backyard either—I could have one right in the middle of my home.

'Don't laugh', I said to my architect, 'but here's what I want'.

I got the home and the slide I wanted. They are emblematic of the power of being clear about intentions.

INTENTIONALITY AND YOUR PRACTICE

Being intentional about what you really want in a home, a living room or anywhere else in your life is the best strategy for getting it. This strategy also applies to your healthcare practice.

You can default to engaging in the pre-existing sickness care model: over-indexing one-to-one visits and constantly coming up with new things to give your patients to take. That's one option, and unfortunately, it's the most popular choice. Or you can be intentional and choose to become a clinician entrepreneur who builds your own version of health and wellness. This second option comes with major perks. It allows you to build a practice around your personal life and values. Instead of starting with limitations, you dream big and create the practice that makes you want to get out of bed in the morning. The profession that reminds you of why you got into healthcare in the first place. The life where you're in control, instead of being controlled by a business model that impacts your ability to deliver care effectively, efficiently and in tune with your life.

This is what intention is all about: knowing what you really want out of your business—and what you want out of life—and having clarity around what will get you there. Clear intention empowers you to break free from the confines of limiting beliefs and gives you an entirely new outlook on your business, your finances and your life.

UNCOVERING YOUR INTENTIONS

Before you can apply this strategy and act on your intentions, you have to discover what they are. This is harder than you might think, especially for practitioners. We went through years of training that entailed following other people's directions and not making mistakes. We focused on caring for patients, but no one taught us how to care for ourselves. Yet, how we build and operate our practices impacts our lives in dramatic ways. We can work too many hours for too little money and burn out. Or we can choose a better way.

Think about your intentions. What is your dream practice? What does it look like, feel like? Put all limitations aside, and envision it.

Does it include helping patients who come to you as a last resort? Patients who have been on their own long, unhealthy path? Or are you working with people on an ongoing basis to improve their health? Are you seeing too many patients, yet feeling as if it doesn't make a difference for most? Or delivering care to more people than you ever imagined, in less time, for more money, and being energized in the process?

If you want the energized option, keep reading. I want to teach you about Entrepology.

ENTREPOLOGY

Much of our lives are built on pre-determined factors defined by a sort of 'template'. We choose the university template, the university-marriage template or the university-career-and-maybe-marriage template. Within each template are other templates, like the one that tells us exactly how to succeed in university and, later, how to run a practice. The curriculum of the healthcare practice template includes a message of positivity: *You, as a healthcare provider, have chosen one of the most honourable professions on Earth. You are about to head out into the world and make a lasting impact. You will also be able to live well in the process (though we won't tell you how to do that—you'll have to figure it out for yourself).*

That's what I was told anyway. Like you, I believed it. I wanted to do good in the world and have a lasting, positive impact. What I didn't understand at the time was how flawed the current methodology was for doing so. The templates were antiquated, based on a pathogenic, transactional model of care. They did not include models to leverage technology, and they inflated the importance of one-to-one visits for every facet of care delivery. They negated the care structure that is the hallmark of Naturopathic and Functional Medicine practices: longer visits, individualized protocols and a patient audience longing for a lasting outcome.

Regardless of your speciality—your *-ology*—there will always be an important piece omitted from the template your school handed you. Where you went to school, the instructors you had, your plans after attaining your credentials—none of these matter. Because the most critical lesson isn't included in any medical training. It's another -ology that I call *Entrepology*.

I created the term 'Entrepology' out of necessity, formed out of a desire to fill the gaps I saw in my own career and gaps in my personal life that formed due to those professional ones.

Entrepology is a study of entrepreneurship at its core. It examines the confluence of entrepreneurial skill, the health of high performance and the mindset of achievement. It takes everything we have been taught to view as a successful practice and career and adds to it the most important aspects of your life. This system was designed to allow the practitioner to help more people, have a greater impact on their patients' lives and create a lasting legacy.

This new -ology is a practical method that highlights the parts of our lives that bring us the most personal joy. It provides a framework for thinking about your desires intentionally.

THE ENTREPOLOGY LIFE SYSTEM

Figure 1: The Entrepology Life System represents the eight areas of potential growth and contribution adjacent to the entrepreneurial journey.

I'LL GIVE YOU THE FRAMEWORK,
YOU MAKE THE RULES

New and *exciting* aren't terms typically associated with healthcare. Likewise, perusing your dictionary of medical terminology won't turn up words and phrases like *equity, profits* or *balance sheets.* Those words weren't on your clinical exams. An Entrepologist knows these words, and I want you to familiarise yourself with them. Thinking of yourself as an entrepreneur—an Entrepologist, specifically—is how you begin to see the bigger picture of what your practice could be and how your life can change when you embrace Entrepology.

Entrepology is a framework, not a rulebook. Distinguishing between the two is critical, especially since, as practitioners, we have been trained via rulebooks. For us, diagnoses come by way of specific symptoms, medications are designated for specific problems and specialities are designed to draw lines in the sand between areas of practice.

Those are hard, fast rules, and there is little grey area.

In entrepreneurship, and in Entrepology, there are no rules— only frameworks. Nothing is set in stone. The road travelled is a multi-lane highway with dotted white lines separating lanes. There's room to explore, to try new lanes and experiment with trails not yet followed, or even blazed for that matter.

Compared to healthcare, where the road travelled is a single-lane highway riddled with solid, yellow lines and rumble strips to warn you *never to cross,* the open road of entrepreneurship may seem scary. It might be tough to adapt to the idea that there are multiple paths to a positive result, but once you accept this idea, the concepts, which I'll explain further within this book, will become clearer. You will see how they are achievable for you.

Are you getting anxious thinking about it? Going crazy over the idea of lanes opening up and things becoming less specific? Not to worry, there will still be rules in place. These rules vary from person to person, but they can still be there, acting as your seat belt in the event anything should happen as you start swerving through lanes.

Rules versus frameworks will be an important component to remember as you read on. But once you adopt a rule, commit to following it. You can revisit them regularly and decide whether they still work for you, but if they're important enough to make part of your practice and your life, yet you continue to bend them, then they aren't rules anymore. They stop serving you. I reevaluate my rules every three months. By reviewing and altering, as needed, my strict rules—my solid, yellow lines in the road—I put myself in the best position to make informed decisions that best suit my life, my intentions, and my goals.

Having clarity around these decisions and acting intentionally is how I make progress towards getting exactly what I want and being exactly where I want to be. You can do the same with your own decisions, rules and, of course, *intention*. You'll have an open path and clarity around where you are, where you want to be and how to get there.

To begin, ask yourself the following questions. Take your time and be honest. Put aside any dreams you had in the past and con-sider your life right now, in this moment, and where you want to head. What would make you happy? You need clarity around this to choose your rules.

CHECK-IN

1. How many people do I want to help?
2. In what way?
3. What models of care make this most efficient and economically accessible (group care, online course, podcast, etc.)?
4. Do I have the time (leverage) to make this happen?
5. What are my personal values that I want to infuse into my business?
6. What are the values of my company?
7. What rules do I want to live by?
8. What rules do I want to build my business by?

CHAPTER 2

INCOME AND GOALS

Your *intention* is clear, your rules are in place, and your mind is open to new frameworks. You have put yourself in a solid place to move forward, and the best next step is to look at the one thing that can make or break your business and your life: Your income.

For some reason, our industry doesn't like to talk about money. *I just want to help* is the phrase a majority of practitioners recite. And while it's true, we *do* want to help, we also need to make sure we're rewarding ourselves for our efforts by having clearly defined income goals.

I have watched as entire clinics are built without consideration for financial modelling. Fee structures are routinely set in place, not on the basis of overhead, demand or the value that is being delivered, but in an attempt to match the pricing of a colleague down the street. When we lack intentionality around our incomes and how we will achieve them, we relegate our respective professions to only those in the most financially privileged circumstances.

Your life's work is also a business. It is not a hobby. It's not something you're going to start on the side and hope it makes enough money to cover your bills. Your practice is your career. It's your livelihood. It is the tool with which you can scale your impact. This isn't something that you should pursue with the idea that *If I just start, things will fall into place.*

This idea falls right back in line with the issue being discussed throughout the book thus far: that our training doesn't include anything outside of *This is how you treat a patient.*

Just as goals need to be put in place to determine how many patients you see in a day, the type of patient relationship you provide and the milestones you accomplish by implementing these goals, your income goals need to be defined with the same level of clarity.

Entrepreneurs, even the reluctant ones, are aware of this need for clarity. Before they even decide to start a business, they put together financials, or estimated fiscal statements for the next few years. This allows them to visualise what sort of growth will be needed to attain the monetary goals they aim to achieve. Once doors are open, profit and loss statements are formed and consistently updated, plans are adjusted, balance sheets become critical, and positions are created for employees or associates to be onboarded with the simple task of keeping these documents in order and current.

This is one of the glaring blind spots with clinicians and their offices: there is no set plan to define numbers. Income goals are often created on a whim, lacking the designation and forecasting that goes into every other type of business plan. This makes it much more difficult to know whether or not an office is truly doing well or whether the provider whose name is on the door—or on the lease, loan, or other business agreement—is putting themselves in a better spot or digging themselves deeper into a hole, emotionally and financially. It is hard to provide authentic care over the long term when your work does not provide the compensation you need to support your family and the lifestyle you desire. We will dive deep into the mechanics of monetization later in this book. I will show you that you can help more people through innovation in your offerings. For now, don't get caught thinking that setting a higher income will mean rendering your services inaccessible to most people. I will show you a new model that will enable every-thing to be true at once. Set your intention, and I will show you the way forward.

Practitioners aren't fearful of investing in their professional ambitions; it is that we are often more comfortable investing in the side of our ambitions that we understand, namely our education. Your education places further restrictions on you because the more education you have, the more you have fallen into this practice of borrowing without the immediate burden of having to pay it back. For many, their primary source of 'income' in their twenties was cash from loans. What's more, the longer you remain in the medical education system, the more you delay and shorten your earning years, and you have the added limitation of how medical regulation can restrict the ways you can earn additional income. This puts more risk on you economically, which automatically drives the price of your commodity higher.

And what is your commodity? That's where most providers are unsure.

TIME VS. RESULTS

How do you price your services? Do you base them strictly off of your gut? Off of experience working within other clinics? Do you calculate when a patient arrives, when they leave and the cost of the visit based on time?

These are all common pricing models, but they are limiting. They force you into selling your time and not your strategy. These are the pricing structures we have been told are the only ones available, and they are only doing damage. Pricing your services based on blocks of time prohibits you from moving past a time-for-money model. Time is used to plan your day; it is not what you are 'selling' as a practitioner. What you deliver is more valuable than time; you are delivering strategy.

Whether we deliver our strategy in five minutes or in four hours, the price shouldn't change. There are advisors who I have interacted with for only a matter of minutes, but their experience and advice has added millions of dollars to my business and shortened my timeline for achieving certain goals by years. Similarly, I have worked with patients where the advice and strategy I have provided has transformed their life and added years to their health span. The value we deliver is more nuanced than charging by the hour. People are paying us to deliver them an outcome, not for our time. When a patient checks in at the front desk and sits down in the lobby, they don't start a clock. They want your expertise, your knowledge and the answers they seek to their problems.

People buy our results. They don't buy our time. And until we as an industry begin to realize this, we will be working backwards, fighting the innovation taking off around us as our feet remain planted in the mud.

THE QUESTIONS
WE SHOULD BE ASKING

Tony Robbins shared with me, long ago in an intimate conversation over audiobook, that the quality of your life is tied to the quality of your questions. The typical questions we have been asking when we decide to open our own practice need to be adjusted. We need to alter our mindset—merge our way over those dotted white lines and into another lane to get a fresh perspective. We need to start asking ourselves new questions, and below are some of those preliminary questions to consider.

What do you deserve to earn?

Have you spent years and years of your life sacrificing your time so that you can learn your speciality? That should be included in this calculation. What about the insurance costs associated with the litigious nature of our industry? Have you considered those? What about the fact that you deliver a strategy that changes people's lives for the better? Add that number into your calculations.

THE COST OF CARE

- Physical overhead
- Health and safety requirements
- Health and safety inefficiencies
- The cost of acquisition for new clients
- The cost of your education
- The cost of maintaining your license
- The cost of CE requirements
- The level of risk you incur (financial/procedural)
- The opportunity cost of your time seeing patients
- The toll on your health
- The outcome you promise
- The results you deliver
- Your demand
- The perception of value that you cultivate
- Your niche
- Others...

Figure 2: A list of some of the obvious and not-so-obvious factors that inform the cost of care delivery.

If you struggle to put these factors together, you're not an outlier. In fact, many clinicians fail to be able to truly put together a number that adequately reconciles what they feel they deserve and what they feel comfortable charging.

If you're struggling to come up with a number for yourself, why not take a colleague and think of a number for them? What about that single mother you went to school with who you know needs to live a certain lifestyle to feel like all of her investments were worth it, to put food on the table? What do you think a reasonable number looks like for her? Once you have a clearer vision of what she deserves, then start to factor in your own life circumstances and formulate an estimate for yourself from there.

What would you like to earn?

Now that you have a number that resembles what you feel you *deserve* to earn, think about what you would *like* to earn. Is it more? Less? Is the number exactly the same? None of these are wrong answers, but the idea of knowing what you would *like* to earn needs to be explored.

When calculating your rates, there are multiple factors to consider. Start by thinking about your future. You aren't just thinking about what you *deserve* to earn after obtaining your education and going through your professional training. Now you're thinking about those future plans that you have—families, children, travel, work-life balance. What do you want your life to look like ten, twenty, thirty years from now? What financial goals do you need to strive for in order to make that desired future become a reality?

Why do you want to earn it?

Where, within the Entrepology Life System categories, do you want to invest? Your ongoing growth, whether that be personal or professional? Maybe it's the experiential components of life, philanthropic missions or simply to pay the bills without stress?

It is critical to know why you want to start making this money because it is important to decide where you want to focus your energy. In understanding why you want to earn this money, it changes the energy. Whether it be spiritually, emotionally, physically or any other energy that drives you, knowing this beforehand will allow you to focus and feel better about being able to strive for these financial goals.

When good people make good money, they can do amazing things in this world. And that can continue towards building overall better health for you and the world around you.

CHECK-IN

1. In what ways do I want to grow spiritually, intellectually and emotionally?
2. What are my monetary goals for the next twelve months? Twenty-four months? Thirty-six months?
3. What percentage of my earnings are going towards my means (costs of living) versus my end goals (the impact I want to make)?
4. What do I deserve to earn?
5. What would I like to earn?
6. Why do I want to earn this money?

CHAPTER 3

RELATIONSHIPS, HEALTH AND EXPERIENTIAL LIVING

D o you remember the day you decided you wanted to become a clinician? More importantly, do you remember the day you told your family and friends it was the path you wanted to pursue? How did they react? There was a lot to celebrate, wasn't there? And for good reason: dedicating your career to helping people as a physician, chiropractor, Naturopathic Doctor, or clinician of any stripe is a noble pursuit.

What about the reaction you received when you told your family (and yourself) that you were also an entrepreneur? You held a large vision for contribution as well as, potentially, a considerable student loan burden and a future path without the security of a consistent paycheck or a pension. For many, this announcement (and personal acknowledgement) is met with less enthusiasm. The risk and vision are questioned. Now you are not only managing your own doubt, but you are additionally having everyone else's fears burdened upon you as well.

When you become intentional about what you really want, these rebuts to your announcements and your inner dialogue won't leave you feeling doubtful or with the sense that you are disappointing others with a reckless pursuit. Entrepreneurship is a noble and worthwhile path. For some, it is a natural fit and desire, and for others, it is met with some level of reluctance. Regardless of your feelings about your entrepreneurial journey, unless you have signed a contract of employment with your clinic (rare), *you* are an entrepreneur.

While this journey came easily to me, I appreciate that that is not the experience of everyone. What unites those who walk this path, however, is the opportunity and flexibility that entrepreneurship affords those who engage in its pursuit. The Entrepology Life System is a tool to acknowledge and leverage the entrepreneurial journey for your own growth and capacity for balance. While it is something you could leverage with your clients, we aren't yet at the part where we are discussing what you deliver to patients. We are still establishing who you need to be to create a business and care strategy that maximizes your impact.

Before we delve deeper into the components of the Entrepology Life System, let's check in on how you feel you are performing in each section of the Entrepology Life System.

WHO DO YOU WANT TO BE AS A CLINICIAN ENTREPRENEUR?

INSTRUCTIONS: Without context, just your gut-check, rate the following areas of your life out of 10.

10 = Amazing, 1 = Oh goodness, I should probably look at that.

☐ **PURPOSE**—DO YOU FEEL LIKE YOU ARE WORKING IN ALIGNMENT WITH YOUR PURPOSE?

☐ **IMPACT**—DO YOU FEEL LIKE YOU ARE HAVING THE IMPACT YOU ARE SEEKING TO CONTRIBUTE?

☐ **INCOME**—ARE YOU EARNING WHAT YOU WANT TO BE EARNING AND FEELING IN CONTROL OF YOUR FINANCES?

GROWTH—DO YOU FEEL LIKE YOU ARE EXPERIENCING GROWTH IN EACH OF THE FOLLOWING AREAS? RATE EACH OUT OF 10.

☐ SPIRITUAL

☐ INTELLECTUAL

☐ EMOTIONAL

☐ **RELATIONSHIPS**—HOW WOULD YOU RATE THE STRENGTH OF YOUR PRIMARY RELATIONSHIPS (FRIENDS, CHILDREN, SPOUSE, FAMILY, COMMUNITY)

☐ **EXPERIENCE**—ARE YOU EXPERIENCING THOSE THINGS IN LIFE THAT YOU WANT TO TRY (TRAVEL, ADVENTURE, ETC.)?

☐ **HEALTH**—DO YOU FEEL YOU ARE SUPPORTING YOUR HEALTH THE WAY YOU WOULD LIKE?

☐ **LEGACY**—DO YOU FEEL LIKE YOU ARE BUILDING A LEGACY (FINANCIAL/INTERGENERATIONAL, PHILANTHROPIC, IP)?

Figure 3: Rate your level of personal/professional satisfaction for each category of the ELS. You will learn more about each section in the upcoming chapters. For now, answer from your gut.

RELATIONSHIPS

When you start a business, you need to be *intentional* about what you want in all arenas of your life. Without clear intentions, you cannot set clear boundaries...and your business will take over. Consider yourself warned.

Launching and running a business, whether you are an associate or the clinic owner, is like having another child. Without date nights locked into the calendar and coffees planned with your friends, you can quickly descend into the myopic world of your baby and the occasional shower. With a baby and a business, we can quickly get overtaken by the fires and the to-do list. The opportunity in parenthood and as an entrepreneur is for you to be able to grow and connect with people who are moving along a similar path and who are interested in the potential for deeper growth and connection along the journey. There are five key relationships you need to pay attention to while taking on this new journey: family, friends, children, partner and community. When you are aware and intentional about the influence of your journey on those around you, the potential for meaningful and deepening relationships is limitless.

A special note here on balancing children and entrepreneurship: My husband and I have three girls who are strong, fearless and talented enough to take on the world in any manner they see fit. Our children are everything to us. While they attend an amazing school and have incredible friends, we are also aware that the biggest influence in their life is us. With intention, my journey as an entrepreneur, health advocate, risk-taker and philanthropist can become part of their arsenal of experience as well. Raising kids and building your ideal practice does not have to force a choice; it can be tackled and approached in unison, stacked together.

We want to have time to walk them to school, be available when they get home, spend nights and weekends together and help them with their homework. I, too, take pride in ensuring my family has healthy meals. My goal has always been to be a great parent regardless of my professional pursuits, and this remains my top priority.

I talk about boundaries with family and friends, and boundaries with your children should be no different. If you want to ensure you spend quality time with them, then do it. Block off that schedule where you need. As you create a more leveraged practice, less dependent on you and your time, this is possible, every day. Intention is about asking what needs to be true professionally for you to pick them up from school, cheer them on at their sporting events and be there to talk to them when they've had a tough day.

Entrepreneurship is hard, but it's also liberating. No other job allows you to completely dictate your schedule and work around your loved ones' lives. Thinking outside the box and innovating your offerings to extend beyond the selling of your time is inspired by, not hampered by, prioritizing the relationships in your life.

No other 'job' allows you the opportunity to teach your children about health, self-actualization and the freedom that accompanies self-reliance the way you can as a clinician entrepreneur. At nine years of age, my oldest daughter gave the opening keynote address at one of our live events. She was so nervous, so worried about what would happen. But she faced her fears and felt, early on, the power of stepping up and surrounding herself with an incredible community. Being part of a 'family business' has allowed her to pick up the necessary traits and learn what she needs to know. It enables her to experience this possibility. And now, as a ten-year-old girl, she owns her own dog-walking company. Would she have the skills, mentorship and confidence to start her own business if her mother was putting in fourteen-hour days at the clinic?

HEALTH

I no longer see patients, but when I did, most of them were entrepreneurs. Running my startup alongside my practice, I witnessed firsthand in the entrepreneurial community my unfair advantage over my fellow entrepreneurs. While they were downing their eighth coffee of the day, my brain and my body were available at a moment's notice. Their curiosity about my protein shakes and supplement containers drove a focussed and compliant population through my doors in droves. When they would come in to see me, they would be on edge. Many, if not all, needed to escape the confines of my room and get back to their high-rises or studios to dive back into the grind of building their empires.

For this group of patients, their intake forms reflected a similar story every time...

Their number-one cause of stress? Work and health.

They were all struggling with the same stressful challenges. *How quickly can I scale my business? How rapidly can I expand my team without driving my business into the ground?* These were energetic people. Yet, IBS, anxiety and sympathetic overdrive characterized my clinical findings.

At the same time, I also treated a considerable number of practitioners in my practice. While their motivations for coming in were different, so too was the subtle origin of their stress.

Their number-one cause of stress? Finances and career.

When I dug deeper into the correlation between stress and their career, it wasn't building or scaling that was creating concern. The issue was principally about not having enough cashflow or time to escape the time-for-money rat-race. It was leaving them frustrated, fatigued and guilt-ridden about the resentment they were feeling for their professional choices and the people they served.

I have had patients with varying careers and professions and what I still found was that most people stress about money and health. For us, as clinicians and the ones giving advice on health, it is incredibly ironic to be suffering ourselves, from the stress and burden of running a business modelled after the 'way it has always been done' instead of a business designed to align with our highest values as people and practitioners.

EXPERIENTIAL LIVING

Money, relationships, work, health—you can drive yourself to an unhealthy state of mind just thinking of the whirlwind of thoughts that comes with being an adult and a professional. Take a step back. Think about why you're working so hard—why you picked this path in the first place.

You wanted to help, right? Of course you did. But you can't help people and never help yourself. You need to think about the things you want to do in life. Do you want to travel? Spend more time with the kids? Work less and still have money to live?

What would it look like if you had your cake and ate it too?

Limiting social constructs have taught us that the most common way to enjoy life is to work hard now and set ourselves up for a great retirement. This is the employee model of economic freedom. But why defer? Why wait? The Entrepology Life System will teach you that you can bake a cake, gluten-free, and still get to enjoy a slice. You can work and travel simultaneously. You can work strategically and then come home to a house that has a giant slide.

A few years ago on a wine tour with friends—one that they swore I wouldn't be able to make because they thought I would be too busy—a server told us about a bottle of wine that he had acquired from the vineyard. 'I bought it for thirty-five dollars', he told us, 'and now it's worth over one thousand'. A smile came across his face, and he shook his head. 'My biggest stress now is knowing when I should open it'.

He was trying to determine if the value would go up, down, remain the same or if the wine would taste better with age. 'Do it tonight', our table told him. 'Go home, open the bottle, share it with your wife, tell her how much you love her and enjoy that bottle in this moment'.

Life doesn't have to be about working hard and deferring the things you want to do.

Experiential living allows you to become rich through experiences, not simply money. The experience itself is the goal, not an 'end goal'.

The idea of experiential living colliding with my own reality came on a random Wednesday night following a long day in the clinic. Trying to compartmentalize my life, I was still at the office at eleven o'clock at night, working tirelessly to finish my charts. Frustrated that everything felt 'so hard', I declared to myself that *something needs to change*.

I printed off a blank patient diet diary and used it 'off-label' to capture all the odd tasks I was responsible for in my life: getting the kids ready for school, patient charting, picking up the kids, cooking dinner, cleaning, laundry, grocery shopping—the list went on. After writing them down, I organized them into three categories: what I loved doing, what I didn't mind doing and what I disliked doing. After that exercise, I decided that I would delegate the *don't minds* and *dislikes* to others without consideration for the guilt and 'shoulds' that were circulating in my head.

Do you know what happened next? It opened up so much time for *me* and my ideal life. It created time to spend with my kids, travelling and doing the things I had in my *love doing* column. I realized that how I was showing up to be with my children, my partner, my friends, my family and my community was much more important than the things I was doing for them. Showing up happy and able to be more responsive—rather than sitting on my phone and answering emails—has proven to be much more enjoyable for them too.

If you're looking for ways to eliminate stress, being *intentional* with what you want out of life is important. Eliminate that sabotaging behaviour and those limiting beliefs. Control those relationships, maintain your health and amplify your life experiences. These actions will drive you towards your own healing and growth...not someday, but now. This is the power of intentional entrepreneurship.

CHECK-IN

1. What am I afraid will happen to _____ relationships if I build my ideal business?
2. What are non-negotiables with respect to my relationships at this phase of my life and business?
3. Am I committing to a business model that sacrifices my relationships? If so, why?
4. What are the non-negotiables with respect to my health?
5. Where do I need to commit to growing to add resilience to protect my health (e.g. financial management, resolving past trauma, addressing limiting beliefs)?
6. What do I want out of the experiential side of my life?

CHAPTER 4

PURPOSE, GROWTH, LEGACY AND GOAL SETTING

A s a practitioner, I observed a phenomenon among my patients: some of them experienced an accelerated path to wellness, while others lagged behind.

From a physiological standpoint, these patients were equal. They all had access to healthy foods, enjoyed nutritious meals and exercised regularly. Their physical resumes, so to speak, were generally indistinguishable. Yet, some healed faster. Their health improved. Others, no matter how much guidance they received, progressed more slowly and didn't show improvements at the same pace, or they stagnated completely.

My curiosity was piqued. Intrigued, I looked deeper, beyond the physical and into the psychology of these two cohorts. I asked my patients questions about their lives. What were they doing behind the scenes of their social media? In their careers? One question in particular elicited responses that appeared to be the clear differentiator between the two cohorts: *What is your purpose?*

Those who had experienced a sense of purpose in their life—who could describe it and were living it—were also the people whose health improved the fastest. Patients who struggled to articulate their purpose or the arenas of contribution that aligned to their unique skills stagnated more frequently with their healing and their health overall.

One patient, Mary (not her actual name) was living a beautifully simple, yet full life. She suffered from depression and was slow to heal. I had a hard time understanding the problem. Mary's husband had passed away years earlier, yet she had a job that she enjoyed and strong ties to her community and was on the board at her local tennis club. She also had healthy relationships with her children, who were grown and living on their own. On paper and after a thorough Functional and Naturopathic Medicine assessment, I was coming up short.

Eventually, it clicked. All of the boxes were checked except one: Mary had no sense of purpose. She was busy. She was needed. But she didn't garner a sense of purpose from contributions she was making in the world. For decades, being a mother to her children and a partner to her husband had been her sole purpose. Her life had revolved around them, and any purpose she might have developed in other parts of her life had been set aside. Once they had moved out of the family home, Mary was left feeling purposeless.

The Japanese have a word for this—*ikigai*, pronounced 'ee-kee-guy'. A combination of *iki*, meaning 'life', and *gai*, meaning 'value or worth', ikigai is the confluence of a person's skills and interests—what they're good at and they what love to do. A person's ikigai has the potential to serve as a contribution to society. In addition to providing satisfaction and fulfilment to the individual, other people often benefit from the contribution as well. One of the features of purpose, as I have come to understand it, is that the confluence of skills and what you love to do also need to be able to fulfil a sense of contribution beyond yourself. This differentiates a hobby or passion from purpose. My patients who lived with a sense of purpose were most likely to heal faster and enjoy better health sooner after sickness. In fact, the medical literature is littered in references to the role that 'purpose' can serve in the reduction of recurrent risk for heart conditions, reduced incidence of anxiety and depression and even lessened risk associated with cancer.

A similar phenomenon occurs in practitioners who are stymied in their efforts to move forward in their practices. We may have what appear to be great careers, yet many of us struggle from a lack of purpose or clarity around our 'why'. As I went deeper into studying this dilemma, I discovered other factors critical to our fulfilment.

Like our patients, we too need purpose.

PURPOSE VS. PASSION

Your sense of purpose is what you're good at doing, love to do, and thrive in practicing. It describes the potential mindset of nearly every clinician because we all simply want to help our patients. We are united in our deep-rooted goal to help.

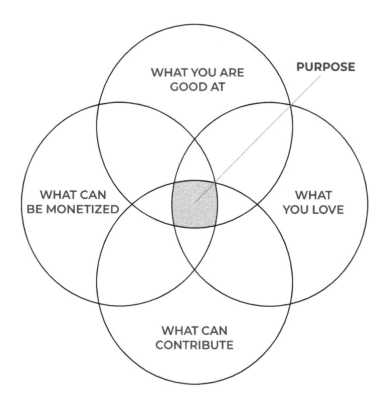

Figure 4: The Entrepology model of purpose. Note the fourth category, the bonus capacity to earn a living through your purposeful work.

The terms 'purpose' and 'passion' are frequently used inter-changeably, yet there is a vast difference in their meanings and the effect each can have on one's health. On a psychological level, purpose is self-sustaining. It engages more than fleeting access to dopamine. Studies looking at the physiological benefits of purpose have even shown that those living in a state of purpose experience curbed levels of cortisol during periods of prolonged stress.[1]

Passion, in contrast, is like burning a candle. It is a more fleeting experience of excitement, and its relentless pursuit often leads to burnout. We can be passionate about our purpose, but passion without purpose frequently results in fatigue and waning interest.

When you take the time to unpack your purpose, you also lay the foundation for growth within your career. I was frustrated with clinical practice and confused about why it wasn't making me happy. I felt guilty that I was afforded a dream job but still felt restless. Until now, the only opportunity for growth outside of the traditional medical infrastructure was to build a clinic. For many, the decision to open a clinic, often with many associates, did not stem from an exercise in business modelling; it was initiated to reflect a desire for challenge and growth. As I gained clarity over my own true purpose and my 'why', I realized that clinical practice was holding me back from my mission to put upstream medicine in the hands of millions. Without making room to understand and unpack my purpose, I too would have copied the models that had been laid out before me. This is the power of committing to finding clarity and intention at the intersection of entrepreneurship and your life. It is a process worth pursuing.

---

1   Nia Fogelman and Turhan Canli, '"Purpose in Life" as a Psychosocial Resource in Healthy Aging: An Examination of Cortisol Baseline Levels and Response to the Trier Social Stress Test', npj Aging and Mechanism of Disease 1, no. 15006 (September 2015), https://doi.org/10.1038/npjamd.2015.6.

GROWTH

As I developed as an entrepreneur, I realized the tremendous opportunity for growth that accompanied my daily experiences. With an expedited frequency, I saw that my personal growth and development did not have to happen outside of my career; it could happen within. And it was occurring whether I liked it or not. Within the Entrepology Life System, growth is embodied in three distinct areas: emotional, spiritual and intellectual.

Emotional growth is being aware of the limitations placed before us and pushing through them. It is the strength that is acquired when we make mistakes, try something new or risk being judged. Emotional growth is the inevitable byproduct of the entrepreneurial journey and any pursuit that requires colouring and playing outside the lines.

Spiritual growth is an optional, advanced move for any entrepreneur. As the limits of your emotional strength are tested, exploration and expansion of your spiritual life remains a daily possibility. As a group disproportionally interested in personal optimization, your community itself becomes a source of spiritual motivation and inspiration regardless of anyone's religious background or proclivity.

Intellectual growth is the unapologetic consequence of five thousand years in school. But there is more to learning than memorizing the Krebs cycle or the insertion point of ligaments and tendons. The intellectual growth that accompanies entrepreneurship is less about facts and defined answers; it leans towards the excitement of system thinking and critical thought. Entrepreneurship is not a straight line, and there is no 'best way'. This is the advantage, not the limitation, and learning to align your thinking strategically is another amazing opportunity for personal expansion.

As you grow, think about what you define as success in that growth. Getting a bad review online could be the end of the world for one practitioner but not for another. Your attitude around growth will set the pace of your acceleration and raise the limits on what you believe you are capable of achieving. Growing yourself and your business may come in fits and starts, growth spurts and intense periods of slow growth, but as long as you're growing emotionally, spiritually or intellectually, you are not standing still. You are expanding your ability to deliver on your purpose.

LEGACY AND GOAL-SETTING

Personal finance. It's what so many of the practitioners I've treated write down as their primary source of stress. More specifically, they shared that their lack of financial acumen was causing disproportionate and unrelenting stress. Most acknowledged that they didn't know what they didn't know. This was driving doubt and emotionally informed decisions about strategic business concerns. They were making good money. They just didn't know how to manage it.

Think about how hard it must be for a healthcare provider making six figures per year to admit that they struggle with finances, both in their personal life and in their business. The average working-class employee may find it hard to believe, but people with good salaries struggle with many of the same financial challenges.

Financial management is not something most people learn in school or anywhere else. Financial hardships affect people at all income levels. Consider the celebrities and athletes who have millions and suddenly fall into bankruptcy. Or the lottery winners who go from financially secure to broke and in debt. Most people think they need more money. What they really benefit from are more money management skills.

Entrepreneurs know they need a financial plan, but this fact seems to elude many healthcare professionals. Regardless of your income, you need a plan for the management of your money.

There are two key types of financial goals that will provide clarity for how you allocate what you earn: means goals and end goals. *Means goals* are your living expenses. Your mortgage or rent. Your car payment. Utility bill and cell phone bill. This is the money that you need to keep a roof over your head, but it's also the money you use to contribute towards those vacations and experiential living.

Your *end goals*, on the other hand, are the funds and financials that you contribute towards ongoing growth. This is the money that you put into your business and into building your legacy. Ends goals can be the ones you set forth for yourself, your family or your patients. This is the money that you invest into your business and your lifestyle that will help you to become better every day.

There is a final category of contribution that should be of consideration conceptually as we discuss finances and the creation of intellectual property more in-depth. The concept is one of legacy. Legacy is the contribution you leave behind. In the context of IMPACT Medicine and the Entrepology Life System, legacy is divided into three categories: financial, intergenerational (health and values) and intellectual. We will unpack all three as we get deeper into the book.

For your patients to be successful in building healthier lifestyles, they will need to step into a state of personal leadership. And the same goes for you and the impact your business can have. The movement from where you are now to where you want to be in the future starts with clarity and intention. You don't have to have the answers to all of these lingering questions now, but it's the intention to uncover the answers that will drive you forward, towards your on-purpose life.

CHECK-IN

1. How would I define my purpose?
2. What skills and talents support my unique capacity for contribution?
3. How would I describe my current relationship with the idea of failure?
4. What are three of my means goals for the next twenty-four months?
5. What are three of my end goals for the next twenty-four months?
6. What is the financial, intergenerational and IP legacy that I want to create over the next ten years? (If you don't understand what I mean by 'IP legacy', don't worry; we'll get into that in the transformational discussion, in Chapter 11.)

PART ONE:
INTENTION—KEY TAKEAWAYS

▶ Only you can set the intention for your life and business. It can happen in consultation with others, but you are the only driver.

▶ The difference between ending up somewhere and ending up where you want is *intention*.

▶ You can help other people and yourself at the same time.

▶ Financial stability is a prerequisite to sustainable and unreserved impact.

▶ Clarity of what you want is what determines your business model, care model and strategic action in your business. Do not copy what others are doing unless you want the same life that they have created.

▶ Entrepreneurship is a rapid accelerant for growth of all kinds.

▶ Intention is not about income. It is about growth, legacy, health, impact and purpose. Income is a secondary byproduct of your primary intentions.

For more IMPACT Medicine resources, visit
impactmedicinebook.com/resources.

PART TWO

MINDSET

'It is not the critic who counts; not the man who points out how the strong man stumbles, or where the doer of deeds could have done them better. The credit belongs to the man who is actually in the arena, whose face is marred by dust and sweat and blood; who strives valiantly; who errs, who comes short again and again, because there is no effort without error and shortcoming; but who does actually strive to do the deeds; who knows great enthusiasms, the great devotions; who spends himself in a worthy cause; who at the best knows in the end the triumph of high achievement, and who at the worst, if he fails, at least fails while daring greatly, so that his place shall never be with those cold and timid souls who neither know victory nor defeat'.

—Theodore Roosevelt

Executing like a boss and living on purpose requires an activation of your self-worth and the deployment of unprecedented courage. This takes work. Confidence does not arrive as a certificate in the mail: 'Congratulations, you have clarity around your intentions; here's the confidence to act on it'! If only. Confidence is the product of courage. It develops from taking courageous action over and over again. Your purpose and your 'why' are bigger than your fear.

Now that you know what you want, it is time to master the second letter in IMPACT, the M. And you guessed it: it stands for Mindset.

A person's mindset, or how they see the world, is influenced by their lived experience. The feelings and emotions we hold towards those experiences reflect the outcomes and memories of the past. When things go well, the feelings are good. When things are a challenge, our physiology reminds us of the past—a built-in warning system that protects us from risk, failure and other uncomfortable sensations. These feelings inform our beliefs, actions and propensity for future action. With influence from those around us, our interpretation and integration of those feelings can result in limiting or enlightened beliefs about our world and our place within it. The relationship towards our past, the emotions it elicits and the beliefs it forms are foundational informants of our mindset. And mindset, my friends, is the set-point and barometre from which IMPACT is formed.

My parents divorced when I was three years old. They shared custody and lived four hours apart. Shuffling back and forth every other weekend, the drive quickly became burdensome, and everyone was eager to find a more efficient solution. It was decided that I would fly, alone, back and forth between Ottawa and Toronto on the quick forty-five-minute flight. For good reason, the thought of getting on a plane by myself was frightening. I was used to travelling with a parent. To make me more comfortable and less afraid, my dad talked to me about flying.

'You should never get nervous on a plane; it's safer than a car', he said. 'If any sort of turbulence happens, look for the reaction of the flight attendants'. He said the inexperienced fliers would get nervous if the plane jostled them a bit and their fear would show on their faces, and they would be a poor judge of what was really going on.

My dad was great at putting me at ease on a plane. He had a logical explanation for anything that could go wrong. I felt safe and confident almost every time I flew because I knew nothing else.

One night onboard a small, nineteen-passenger plane, something finally did go wrong for real. The plane was too small for an actual flight attendant, so the passengers were making guesses as to what was going on. For nearly twenty minutes, the plane had made repeated attempts to move towards the runway, only to turn off course and aim for the tower. There was a dense fog, and people were guessing that it was making the landing unsafe. The plane would descend, then circle around and back up, without touching down. Eventually, the pilot spoke up, announcing over the intercom what was going on.

'We're having trouble getting the landing gear down', he said, 'There's a manual crank, but the fog outside is so dense that when we fly by the flight tower, they can't tell if it's down or not'.

That panic my dad had talked about was setting in with the other passengers. With every fly-by we did, that panic grew louder and became more visible. People around me grabbed their armrests and held on for dear life. Everyone, it seemed, feared the worst. They didn't know what was going to happen. But I did. My dad had told me about these situations. He said that pilots were trained for all types of scenarios, including landing the plane on its belly if the wheels didn't work. *Easy peasy, lemon squeezy, everyone needs to calm down*, I thought. Where was a calm flight attendant when I needed her?

On one such descent, I peered through the window and saw fire trucks and emergency vehicles below, on the tarmac. With each pass, more vehicles and flashing lights appeared. The other passengers seemed to be prepared for the worst, but I remained relatively calm. It was just like my father said it would be, so being afraid didn't enter my mind. I didn't know to be afraid, and so I wasn't.

Eventually, we landed safely, on wheels. After all that chaos and fear, circling back down to the tower to see if it was safe to land, the pilot eventually had to go for it—he had to take a risk. I looked out the window in awe, excited about this potential belly landing my dad had told me so much about. 'Pilots can even land on the water if they need to', he'd said.

The landing gear worked, and the plane rolled down the runway to a safe stop. We were escorted off the plane by relieved airline officials. I was giddy, knowing I had an exciting story to share.

Years later, I appreciate my naiveté. I was aware of the situation but immune to the expected emotional consequences. We all find ourselves in situations we don't expect. Allowing fear to control our thoughts and behaviours is rarely the most constructive approach. Fear prevents us from seeing the most beautiful version of an outcome and keeps us from seeing opportunities and potentially positive results. Fear keeps us safe, not necessarily impactful.

Fear management is a skill we need to bring into our businesses. Stepping outside our comfort zones and taking risks shouldn't scare us. Risks and mistakes are *inevitable* stepping stones towards our greatness. They are not optional, and they are not the end of the world. Whatever happens, it probably won't crash the plane.

CHAPTER 5

THE RELATIONSHIP BETWEEN COURAGE AND CONFIDENCE

magining worst-case scenarios and most-likely scenarios is one way to manage your fear. Strategically tapping into your 'why' and your reason for showing up is another. Nothing in life is guaranteed. But you have not come this far, *only* to come this far.

As practitioners, we make decisions with the latter mindset all the time. We were literally trained to consider the worst-case scenario all the time. We worry more about hedging ourselves against the potential downfalls rather than attacking risk and reaping the reward. The human brain is wired to prioritize our protection from the downside, rather than to encourage a ten-fold increase in our potential. We, like trained pilots landing in the fog, are who everyone looks to when they become aware of their own mortality or physiological limitations. It's no wonder we try to avoid risk whenever possible.

Consider the missed opportunities and hedged outcomes in our businesses and our lives when we are motivated by risk mitigation versus the pursuit of reward and impact. What are we leaving on the table? Financial freedom? Time freedom? Growth of our practice? Making more impact while working less hours? Experiences or more time with our kids and families? These are all positives, yet we avoid them, worried that we might make the wrong choice, look foolish or simply not succeed on the first attempt.

Moving ahead in life and in your business is not something solved by time, and it is not reserved for those who are naturally confident. Confidence is a byproduct. It is earned. We need a mindset shift that highlights courage and confidence over fear because each day that we talk ourselves out of taking action, we move further from where we want to be. Stop negotiating with your potential.

If your goal is to open up more of your time and to achieve financial independence through your practice, then going through the same routine isn't going to get you there. Removing a limiting and fearful mindset will.

This psychology of courage over fear, leading to confidence over scepticism, is how we begin to change. We must acknowledge our own fears and distrust, then train ourselves to embrace courageous action every day. Courageous decisions and actions lead to a state of competence through repeated experience and execution. It's unsexy and quiet, and it gets the job done ... in the dead of night.

Competence is the secret sauce from which confidence is born, hidden in plain sight.

DON'T WAIT AROUND FOR CONFIDENCE

We practitioners and entrepreneurs have a weird relationship with confidence. It's as if we are waiting for it to come in the mail. We think that someday it will be handed to us, as if we don't have to actively acquire it. We wait for permission to have it, like a patient waiting for us to write them a prescription or provide them with a lifestyle change to improve their health.

This behaviour should come as no surprise. Waiting for approval, for permission, for the chance to move forward is what we've been doing for years:

You are now qualified to start kindergarten, first grade, second…

You are now qualified to become an undergraduate.

You are now qualified to enter your post-graduate clinical training.

You are now qualified to practice _____.

Do you see a pattern? We've become so used to waiting for the go-ahead from somebody else—usually a third-party, faceless body—that we can't change what we're doing, or move to the next stage, without it. We need to find the confidence to take that next step on our own, without looking around for someone to tell us that we're qualified to do so. We need courage and confidence to take risks.

That confidence isn't coming in the mail. You can't take a test and get a certificate that qualifies you as confident enough to take on the world. Only you can trigger the courage that enables the confidence to come. Delivering care and growing a business, you are the person in charge. You're the one who says you're qualified. If you are afraid to do that, then you face an even greater risk, the risk of remaining stagnant, in life and in your career.

CONTINUUM OF CONFIDENCE

Dan Sullivan, Founder of Strategic Coach and a thought leader for entrepreneurs, has a concept called 'The 4 Cs Formula'.[2] I participated in his programme and found his thinking and frameworks extremely valuable. His continuum comprises four Cs that facilitate access to a more confident mindset.

Courage

In Sullivan's programme, the first step in acquiring confidence is having courage. Per the Continuum of Confidence, you can be courageous at any time. Brené Brown's advice on the matter is that you have to be able to step into the ring.[3] In other words, you have to put yourself out there.

Being courageous isn't something you should wait for. *The timing is never right*. It is a decision. One you are capable of making today.

Commitment

The second C is commitment. Once you have committed to being courageous, you need to hold yourself accountable towards immediate forward momentum.

---

2   Strategic Coach, accessed August 26, 2022, https://www.strategiccoach.com/.

3   *Brené Brown: The Call to Courage*, directed by Sandra Restrepo (2019; Netflix), streaming.

Commitment is hard, especially when the action we need to take feels so esoteric. We open our doors and put up a website, but if we don't see immediate results, we give up. I've heard it so many times: *I've tried everything, and nothing works.*

Business is a long game, not a short one. If you've been in business for just six months, you haven't tried everything. It's like a patient who comes to you after following your diet and exercise guidance for a month and still hasn't lost twenty pounds or lowered their cholesterol: *I did everything you told me to do, and none of it works.*

You need to make a deep commitment to the craft. A *deep* commitment, like you're in it for the long haul, which you are. Once you experience some success, the ability to stay committed becomes much easier. Surprisingly, you can use the failures to strengthen your commitment too because, as you fail and learn, you develop the next C: competence.

Competence

Competence is like a wave of momentum that you develop through having the courage to act and the commitment to stick with it. That wave carries you to a place of competence, where suddenly, without even being conscious of the transformation, you realize that you're really good at something you couldn't do before. Competence's wonderful side effect is—you guessed it—confidence.

Confidence

Now, after all that courage, commitment and competence, confidence will come your way. You didn't wait for someone to bestow it upon you or suddenly pronounce you confident. You worked for it. You earned it. You *claimed* it. Be proud of that achievement.

Confidence feels so good, yet, as practitioners, we must beware a false sense of confidence that pervades our field. False confidence, in this case, may be labeled more accurately as 'misapplied confidence'. This is the false confidence that happens when we overlook competence and place too much importance on our qualifications.

THE CE TRAP

Our qualifications are often based on education and credentials. I'm not downplaying a good education or advanced skills, but practitioners have a bad habit of taking it too far. Rather than build their competence, confidence and their business, they get caught in the CE Trap.

The CE (or CME) Trap is the Continuing Education Trap. It's when you keep repeating what you already know: how to be a student. After twenty-plus years in school, we know the ropes. Opening a practice and owning the responsibility of building a practice really takes us down a notch. It challenges us in new ways. It triggers doubt. It picks at our confidence. When we feel down and unsure of what to do, it is human nature to turn to a model or skill where we have known success—in this case, school. *If I get just one more credential, people will come*, we tell ourselves. This is the CE trap. It lures us towards what we know. It makes us feel good about our capacities, but it does not directly move our business or our impact forward.

My mother, a drama teacher, would say, 'You need to stop rehearsing the scene you already know'. She was talking to her acting student, but the sentiment applies here as well. Stop rehearsing that same scene. Stop going back to the conventional ways of progressing in your career because you're afraid to try new things. Degrees, certifications and adding more letters after your name will only move your impact so far. Those letters will do very little to move your business forward. It is governed by the law of diminishing return.

The CE Trap accomplishes a few things. It puts you further in debt, it distracts you, and it delays your real progress. It feels like you're doing something, but the reality is that you're simply avoiding the action your business requires—action like marketing yourself and your care methodology, teaching through social media, designing your brand or establishing systems within your business. Continuing education has an important time and place. Ensure you are not overindulging in an area of your career where you 'know' how to feel successful.

Let's get this straight: if you have the courage to dedicate months, even years, of your life to another certification, incurring thousands of dollars in debt that you will have to pay back, surely you have the courage to post on social media! Go back to the four Cs: Courage. Commitment. Competence. Confidence. You have it in you to step into the ring today—I promise.

CHECK-IN

1. Where am I feeling most confident in my career?
2. Where am I feeling the least confident? Why?
3. What impact do I want to have in people's lives with my training and expertise?
4. What are three courageous steps I can take right now to move forward in the area where I am feeling least confident?

CHAPTER 6

THE ANATOMY
OF LIMITING BELIEFS

We all have patients who visit us repeatedly for the same ailments. Their treatment plans never seem to work, and so they show up, month after month, with upturned hands asking, 'What else can I try?'

Chances are high that you have a number of patients who can't seem to improve their health. Yet, you have even more patients whose health problems have been eased or eliminated, thanks to your strategy, empathy and expertise.

The human brain is trained to believe that a treatment plan associated with a diagnosis will work. The more a person believes this, the better the chances the plan will work. Similar to a placebo effect, when a patient has confidence in their practitioner, the outcome is usually easier to achieve.

Limiting beliefs are not confined to your career. They affect us in all facets of life. Our beliefs are a higher function of the brain, triggered by experience and imprinting, often when we are quite young. When triggered, they elicit activity in the amygdala, the hypothalamus and the hippocampus. That advanced brain activity and the cascading neurochemistry are the physiological blueprint of our beliefs—limiting or growth-provoking.

Many of our core beliefs and attitudes were introduced to us by the time we were six to seven years old. Your views on politics, money, family and risk were highly influenced by your family of origin at an early stage of life. When our parents told us to 'be careful' or 'don't do that' to protect us from dangerous or uncomfortable situations, their words stuck. How we were raised, then, set the stage for just how limited or expansive our beliefs were and would become. When little girls are praised for being good and not speaking up, they are conditioned at a young age to question raising their voice. For clinicians, our beliefs and conditioning often supported us well in school. We aimed for perfection, we paid attention to detail, and we learned that hard work paid off. *As clinician entrepreneurs, the conditioning of school is often detrimental to our success. Perfectionism holds us back, risk management is a necessity, and our beliefs around money will be routinely triggered.*

How we are raised can limit, or free, our mindset. It sets our beliefs, which remain with us as we grow into adults. We aren't stuck with them, though. Thoughts and beliefs, through decisions, can be changed.

CHANGING YOUR BELIEFS

We all aim to avoid discomfort. That avoidance is the reason patients come to us in the first place. If they have an illness or injury, they want quick relief. Fast comfort is preferable to even a few minutes of uneasiness, fear or pain.

In the book *90 Seconds to a Life You Love*, author Joan Rosenberg claims that we spend a considerable amount of our time and energy to simply avoid ninety seconds of discomfort.[4] She explains how our neurochemistry won't allow for more than a minute and a half of uncomfortable feelings, driving us to seek solace, often before any real change or growth can begin.

By giving in to our neurochemistry, we often avoid critical opportunities for growth. When you consider all the years of schooling you endured to have the impact you have dreamt of, how does ninety seconds of discomfort compare? It's a mere drop in the bucket in the big world of change and growth. If we could ignore our wiring and make the conscious effort to endure a teeny bit of misery or, really, just being uncomfortable, we might come out on the other side a different person with a new life full of potential.

Going from avoidance to a place of acceptable discomfort takes practice, but you can make that *choice*. The growth that comes from pursuing your dreams and capacity for impact is unlike the growth we experienced at school. This is next-level learning and expansion.

---

4   Joan I. Rosenberg, 90 Seconds to a Life You Love: How to Master Your Difficult Feelings to Cultivate Lasting Confidence, Resilience, and Authenticity (New York: Little, Brown Spark, 2019).

Leaning into discomfort and choosing *you* is exactly what we are asking our patients to do as they lean into better health. Stepping outside your comfort zone, making missteps, even finding failure —these are prerequisites for impact. Your limiting beliefs can and should be overcome.

Addressing my belief system is a daily practice in my personal and professional life. My creativity as a clinician and entrepreneur alike are predicated on my ongoing acknowledgement of the parametres informing my thoughts and strategy. I am committed to stepping outside of my comfort zone on a daily basis, and as a supportive practice, I start nearly every morning with a two- to four-minute cold plunge. The sub-forty-degree water and ice mix was very uncomfortable the first time I tried it, but eventually, my body adapted to the temperature, and I can now sit submerged and remain calm. It is a time where I remind myself what I am capable of. It keeps me focussed on my day, and it reminds me that hard things are possible when we practice.

Growth happens when you put yourself in uncomfortable situations and witness, for yourself, what you are truly made of. I'm not proposing you draw a cold bath and throw in a bucket of ice—or maybe I am. I *am* simply suggesting that growth and impact happen outside your box of comfort. We were not designed to remain comfortable; we were designed to withstand pressure. We were designed for growth. Your version of a cold plunge may be going live on social media or promoting yourself to prospective patients or raising your rates. To avoid the stress and overwhelm of running a business, many turn instead to what they know: school. We (I've done it too) lean back into credentialing ourselves just a little more, in the hopes that more clinical education is a backdoor entrance to the stage of business success. It's not. It's a trap, governed by your need to stick with what you know. Like every challenge you have taken on in your life, this is simply the next frontier... and IMPACT Medicine is your guide. Hop into your proverbial cold plunge, and your potential for growth may surprise you.

LIMITED BELIEFS AFFECT YOUR BUSINESS

Your brain and your physiology—your physical self—enjoy a partnership that can help or hinder you. Those beliefs that are wired into our brains help us make decisions as adults, and the more credence and validation we offer those beliefs, the more hardwired they become. You can, as you know, alter that physiology. By choosing a new narrative, taking new action and accumulating new evidence, neuroplasticity will alter your feedback loop, updating what you believe about yourself and your potential. Remaining stuck in beliefs and behaviours that limit your growth can have a negative effect on your ability to grow your practice and your impact.

Consider the following beliefs and how they might be holding you back:

I'm not good with money.

I'm not good at speaking in front of people.

I just want to help people with the things I went to school to learn.

What if you choose to overwrite those beliefs with new ones like these?

I can learn to master my finances.

When I gain clarity around my purpose and practice articulating that purpose, I have the opportunity to teach others how to access better health.

I want to help as many people as possible with the things I learned from school.

Now this next part I say with love, but female practitioners and entrepreneurs experience higher, disproportionate incidences of limiting mindsets when it comes to business finances, and sometimes their personal finances as well. They feel as if dealing with money is not one of their core competencies, and so they should focus on what they've been trained to do and hand the finances off to someone else. This is often rooted in how we have been socialized and the exposure we were granted to money in our youth. The consequences of these origins are not unique to the industry of healthcare and wellness. As of 2021, there are over thirteen million female lead businesses in the United States, and they contribute to over $1.9 trillion in revenue. Despite these numbers, there remain universally troubling figures: based on data from 2018, when seeking financial assistance, women seeking bank loans received funding 31 per cent less than their male counterparts and 70 per cent were denied funding outright.[5] Similarly, men are 60 per cent more likely to successfully win seed or angel investment capital for new

---

5   Rohit Arora, 'The Lending Gap Narrows for Women Business Owners, But It's Still 31%Less than for Men', CNBC, March 7, 2019, https://www.cnbc .com/2019/03/07/the-lending-gap-narrows-for-women-business-owners -nationwide.html.

ventures.[6] The societal bias towards women is real, and we will change that story.

After my transition from the Integrative Health Institute, I worked for two years as the CEO of a digital media startup alongside my practice. While we boot-strapped for the first eight months, there came a time where we needed to seek additional investment. I flew to Ottawa to make my pitch. I meticulously prepared the numbers, the slide deck and the pitch. I walked into the room confident and prepared to make my case. But no one was looking at my deck or listening to what I had to say. 'How are you going to manage the business and your new baby', someone finally asked. I was six months pregnant. 'The same way I handled it with my first two', I replied.

Your identity as 'I'm just not a numbers person' stops today. Why are men in our industry earning more? What needs to be true for you to champion parity and financial growth for yourself and others?

You don't need to be a finance expert to run a successful practice, but you need to look under the hood with confidence. If you can read blood work, you can handle the details of your financial statements. Money, like the body, is simply a metric in a complex system. Once you learn the vocabulary, simple experience will build your confidence with the meaning. Knowing your numbers is about acquiring the capacity to confidently speak to your accountant, bookkeeper (yes, you need both) and business and life partners about your priorities, strategy and goals. As the CEO of your

---

6   Alison Wood Brooks et al., 'Investors Prefer Entrepreneurial Ventures Pitched by Attractive Men', PNAS 111, no. 12 (March 2014): 4427–4431, https://doi.org/10.1073/pnas.1321202111.

business, *you* are the one who gets to call the shots. You don't have to ask permission or abdicate the financial responsibility to anyone. You *get* to own it.

We'll delve deeper into self-authorization in Chapter 8, but it's an important concept here too. Self-authorization is the act of standing in your own authority without the need to ask for permission or repeated insight from others to make decisions in *your* life and business. It is a critical developmental milestone as an entrepreneur, and it is unlocked through courageous, committed action. You don't have to wait for permission to learn about money, and you don't need a degree in finance to have productive discussions with your accountant. You are an entrepreneur, and this is your mission. Put one foot in front of the other, step into the ring, walk into that zone of discomfort and prepare to amaze yourself as the person who comes out the other side.

CHECK-IN

1. List the core beliefs you were exposed to when you were young as it relates to money.

2. How much money would you like to receive as income from your business each year?

3. What do you need to learn to have a greater sense of confidence with your money?

4. What beliefs do you need to address to drive a stronger relationship with money?

5. Do you have a bookkeeper managing your business's financial tracking?

CHAPTER 7

MANAGING IMPOSTOR SYNDROME

We humans have a known bias for underestimating our own abilities while overestimating everyone else's. (Read that again.) We assume that other practitioners and their practices have none of the problems that we're dealing with, like too few patients, too much work, too low rates and no work-life balance. To the outsider looking in, everything looks peachy; they are masters at marketing, they know just what to say, or they are financially stable. Those of us who actually achieve an enviable level of success may feel like pinching ourselves to see if it's real or a dream. Did we earn our position, our wealth and our state of fulfilment, or are we just pretending? Often, there's a period of adjustment where we feel like imposters.

When we think of successful business people and innovators, names like Richard Branson, Oprah Winfrey, Elon Musk and Sara

Blakely come to mind. The divide between us and them seems massive—as if we're here, down on Earth, while those people are excelling up there in the stratosphere. If you think I'm going to tell you that's a limiting belief, you're correct. The aforementioned entrepreneurs didn't just walk onto the scene as billionaire business owners. They started out on the same side of the fence as most other entrepreneurs. A key differentiator in this group is their willingness to take big risks and get up quickly when they fall.

After three years of working with practitioners, I knew I needed to do something bold to add income and scale my influence. With a background in theatre and a deep desire to change the way my industry gathered and inspired one another, I knew I wanted to run an event...a big event. I had done this before, but not nearly at this scale and definitely not in front of my colleagues. Simultaneous to this decision, I was living in a rented apartment while our house was gutted as part of a renovation gone mad. With nothing but mounting debt, deep fatigue (I moved four times in four months with three kids under six) and a desire to change the quality of my impact, I took big, bold action and a huge personal risk on a significant personal vision. The only thing I knew for sure was that the event would be called Impact LIVEs.

Researching others in the industry who organized similar events, imposter syndrome set in: *These people have been doing this for years. They're known, and they make a lot more money than I do. Who am I to compete with the pros?*

I reconsidered the conference. Maybe I should forget all about it and just stick with my usual programmes. They were doing okay—why change things up? I had another thought too: *I'm comfortable with my programmes, and holding a conference is going to cause me some serious discomfort. At least ninety seconds worth—probably much more!*

Dr. Joan Rosenberg was right. I was avoiding short-term discomfort for long-term benefits, and I had to get over it. Slow and steady had done its job. It was time to go big and bold. It was the only way to get past my imposter syndrome, and the best way to make a dramatic impact in a short amount of time. I immediately called the best event space in the city to request a tour.

A woman showed me around, and I was blown away. The space was perfect—not some windowless conference room in a downtown hotel but big and airy, with huge windows overlooking the city.

'How much is it?' I asked, excitedly.

The woman replied, 'It will depend on the extent of the programme, but to hold the space, we will require a $30,000–deposit today'.

I didn't have the money, but something inside made me say, 'Do you take credit cards?'

I booked it, still wondering how I was going to pull it off financially. The total cost for the room would be nearly $100,000. I also had to hire keynote speakers, arrange food and pay for all of the IT. I had never done something this irresponsible and important at the same time. My only option was to bet on myself.

Throughout the entire planning phase, I continued to fight imposter syndrome. Still, I recruited speakers, promoted the event and started selling tickets. People were buying them, and as each day passed, I grew more confident. Impact LIVEs was going to be a success.

I managed my imposter syndrome, sold two hundred tickets and threw one heck of an inaugural event.

RISK VS. REWARD

One of the fastest ways to get over imposter syndrome is to do something that makes you really uncomfortable. Get up in front of a crowd and give a speech or a presentation. Record videos of yourself speaking and post them online. Plan a massive conference. Do something that will help others, while making yourself uncomfortable. Take a risk, and put yourself out there.

If it's the risk that's holding you back, figure out which kind of risk is scaring you. Is it financial or emotional? It could be both. When I set up that conference, the financial risk was huge, but I did it anyway, and I didn't tell anyone about it at first—not even my husband. This was my risk to take and to manage.

The emotional risk was pretty big too. Handing over my credit card for the deposit, I'd be lying if I said I wasn't sweating a little ... a *lot*. It was scary, but it was thrilling too. Because I was starting to believe that I could pull it off. I could hold a successful event that helped other people and brought me closer to my goals.

There is a frequent association between entrepreneurship and risk, and it's probably deserved. People who want to start their own businesses tend to have a higher tolerance for risk. They might even thrill to the idea of standing so close to the emotional edge. Practitioners don't always feel as if they're part of that crowd. We mistake risk with a state of stress destined to harm our health or threaten our lifestyle. We often don't consider that the slow and steady model of seeing one patient at a time, day in and day out, doesn't win the race. It is actually a slow war of attrition, depleting time and energy over time. Regardless of your model of care, you need to approach your business with intention and recognize that you are in the driver's seat. With this book and these frameworks, we are mitigating the risk by not heading into business, riding blindly on the coattails of good intention.

Yet, the path to impact and the life you are capable of living will not be void of risk. Consider for a moment how taking a risk can allow you to see many more patients and influence more lives. It's a manageable risk for a practitioner committed to helping patients, while growing their practices and being fairly compensated for their worth. And, while you lean into this potential for yourself, you will be assisting others to do the same. Investing in their health, sharing vulnerabilities and changing the way they live their lives is a significant financial and emotional risk for patients as well. You are not walking this choice alone. You will be leading from experience every single day.

PURPOSE DRIVEN

If you're still struggling with imposter syndrome, consider that what you're doing isn't about you; it's about your purpose. Whatever it is that you're trying to accomplish is surely important enough to push forward, past fear, past a lack of confidence, past second-guessing yourself and what you have to offer. Can you imagine if people stopped doing interviews because Oprah does them so well? Or if all the restaurants closed down because the chefs didn't want to compete with Gordon Ramsey? The world would be a dull place without the rest of us in it to lend our voices, talents and our time.

When you start to get those feelings, that sense that you're uncomfortable and maybe you're not quite up to a thing, and that little voice in your head says to shrink back, you need to push back. When you get that feeling and hear that voice, get excited. It's the first sign that you're doing something grand. It is a trail marker for impact living. You're innovating, growing and making someone's life better. You're adding value to the world.

Get clear on your purpose. Put it out there. Work to make it happen, and don't shy away from doing what needs to be done. You're no imposter—you're the real deal. The world just hasn't seen you yet, and it doesn't know what you can do. Get out there and show everyone that you're not afraid to step over the fence and into the land of entrepreneurial greatness.

CHECK-IN

1. If you knew no one would judge you and that you could not fail, what would be the next move you make in your career?
2. What situations, if any, trigger imposter syndrome for you?
3. If you had 20 per cent more self-esteem, would it change the decisions you make in your life and business? In what way?

CHAPTER 8

BECOMING YOUR OWN GURU

Self-Authorization

I remember the first time I heard someone speak about the control that authority has in our lives. The woman, a guest on my podcast, talked about how we are introduced to authority as children. We are trained to seek authority from outside ourselves, from our parents, our teachers and our coaches. The woman noted that as part of healthy development, we will transition from our parents fulfilling a primary role of authority to it being transferred to ourselves. Only that is not what my brain said. It filled in the blank before she could: *we transfer authority from our parents to our partners*. Houston, we have a problem. I stopped dead in my tracks. I don't remember what I asked her next. I was dealing with my own existential crisis around self-authorization.

How was I so wrong? What was going on in my subconscious?! If I assumed that we hand authorization to our partners, were other women having the same thought? I was experiencing exactly what she was warning against—the tendency to continue assigning authority to other people, past childhood and well into adulthood. I recognized my thought for what it was: a limiting belief that had to be eradicated.

STOP WAITING FOR PERMISSION

Let me check with my business partner. Let me check with my spouse. Let me check with so-and-so.

We hear these phrases from our patients way too often. Instead of owning authorization over their lives, they've transitioned it from their parents to another person. Even with something as personal as healthcare, people seek the permission of others beyond their practitioner.

Similarly, people—including practitioners—wait for authorization to do something with their business. It's not like they're waiting around for it; most often, people don't even think about the fact that they could be authorizing themselves to take action. As professional students, we were trained to wait for direction. We were provided the criteria for success, and we were told when to start and stop. This new role has no direction and knowing where to start often stops people in their tracks. They could be propelling themselves forward but are paralysed with either a lack of action, a lack of decision-making or both.

If you are growing a business, momentum is your best friend. If you don't know what to do next, you need to find out *who* to ask. No one is going to show up and tell you what to do. You don't need to know what to do, but you need to decide that you are willing to find out. You know your vision for impact and your industry better than your partner or your parents. While outsiders can serve as sounding boards, the final decision needs to live with you. As a business owner (solo practitioner, associate and clinic owner alike), you have the ultimate authority to make all of the decisions surrounding *your* business. Even if it is not yet making money.

Seeking permission to execute on an idea from somebody who doesn't know your business is almost destined to result in that idea being stopped in its tracks. Those you seek permission from may not be entrepreneurial. Their tolerance for risk will be informed by different metrics and experience. By seeking advice from somebody else who hasn't studied your business or your industry as thoroughly as you have, you aren't giving the idea a fair advantage. As an entrepreneur, you need to have decisiveness. It is your job to have clarity on the outcome you are looking to achieve and to assemble the requirements for it to come to fruition. Be the one who is confident enough to make decisions without seeking outside permission.

DECISIVENESS IS A KEY ATTRIBUTE OF ENTREPRENEURS

Indecision is a symptom of poor self-authorization. Becoming decisive is a choice that takes practice. You can consciously begin to authorize your own decisions, instead of seeking outside permission. This action may take more courage and confidence than you have right now, but you can get there.

You can also set rules for yourself around decisions. When I make big decisions around shiny things in my business, I deploy a twenty-four-hour rule for my decision-making. If somebody is attempting to sell me something that I find incredibly alluring, I will be very clear with them about my rule up front—*I think this is great, but I need twenty-four hours to think about it.* Unless I walk into an event or conversation knowing exactly what I am looking for, which I often do, I avoid making decisions when my dopamine levels are pulsating through my system.

The twenty-four-hour rule removes the emotion and allows me the time and space to make a decision based on strategy, not feelings.

What information do you need to know to make the most informed decision? This is what is most important to know. Once you have all the information on hand, having the confidence to make this decisive choice on your own becomes much easier.

I Will...

…*harness my courage.*

…*record my limiting beliefs.*

…*do the fricking work.*

…*use imposter syndrome as my compass.*

…*practice self-authorization daily.*

YOU CAN STILL HAVE A SOUNDING BOARD

Being decisive is important, but don't overlook the idea of a sounding board or advisors to turn to for support. Many entrepreneurs are admittedly weak in certain areas of their businesses, and they delegate. When it comes to finances, for example, business owners don't always know all the ins and outs of bookkeeping and accounting, so they turn to a CPA for help. I will never tell you not to lean on a CPA or another financial expert. However, you are the captain of the ship. Check in with the crew and team members you trust, but ultimately, you need to set the course and speed. Don't be tempted to rely on the advice of others for important decisions that you are in a much better position to manage. Seek out mentors and fill your learning gaps. But never hand off control of those important business decisions to someone else.

I once had a meeting with a client whose husband showed up on the call—and *only* he showed up on the call—because he knew more about her finances. I was mortified.

Self-authorization takes practice. Since handing off decision-making in our lives has been ingrained in us as children, we have to consciously change our way of thinking and our behaviours. With practice, self-authorization becomes more natural and eventually automatic.

Be courageous. Step out into that new world and take on your decision-making efforts. Let go of the limiting belief that you need the permission of others and improve your business like only you know how to do. Once you have that control over your decisions and your business, you can focus on the reason you got into medicine in the first place: to serve people who need you and can benefit from the better health that you can deliver.

CHECK-IN

1. Where are you lacking self-authorization?
2. What needs to be addressed so that you can step into a position of stronger decision-making?

PART TWO:
MINDSET—KEY TAKEAWAYS

▶ Rehearsing scenes you already know does not improve the quality of the show. Stop searching for confidence in the areas of your professional life you have mastered and start working on the scenes that are holding you back.

▶ Courage, not confidence, is how you start.

▶ Your mindset is *the* most important determinant of your business success and your sole responsibility. This part of your work is never ending.

▶ Your limiting beliefs have a loud voice, but they are not the most important opinion.

▶ Your job as the CEO of your business is to learn and confront what is necessary to effectively self-authorize as a leader. Stop seeking permission from others.

▶ Imposter syndrome is a normal part of growth. Lean into it.

▶ Expecting things to be easy is a limiting belief. Hard work, calculated risk, failure, windfalls, big falls, ease, vulnerability and success will all be part of your journey. They are one big entrepreneurial family, and you can't have one without the other.

▶ Decisiveness is a critical entrepreneurial skill. Address the mindset work required to make this a feature you practice in your leadership journey.

For more IMPACT Medicine resources, visit impactmedicinebook.com/resources.

PART THREE

P OF PATIENTS (THE PEOPLE YOU SERVE)

'Art is what we call … the thing an artist does.

It's not the medium or the oil or the price or whether it hangs on a wall or you eat it. What matters, what makes it art, is that the person who made it overcame the resistance, ignored the voice of doubt and made something worth making. Something risky. Something human.

Art is not in the … eye of the beholder.
It's in the soul of the artist'.

—Seth Godin

magine your house was on fire. Your kitchen was engulfed, the smoke was spreading, and it was beyond your ability to handle on your own. Once you had fled for safety, the next step is obvious: you would call for help. This is not the moment where you investigate your ideal firefighting unit online. You are not checking the Google reviews, and you are not swayed by the quality of a department's website or firefighting methodology. You dial nine-one-one and gratefully accept the team that arrives first.

But fighting the fire is different from preventing it in the first place. When it comes to fire safety and prevention, each fire station may offer different advice. Fire containment, for example, could be a top priority in rural areas where bonfires are the norm, while proper smoke detector installation might top the list for departments in a crowded city. There's much more open-endedness to the process of fire safety than there is for firefighting, and much of it is formed by people's location, level of knowledge, and in some cases, even their detector aesthetic.

Healthcare is the same. When there is a fire that needs to be extinguished, patients call any doctor. The relief they seek is instant, and they are willing to trade access to the best or to a nuanced approach in favour of expediency. The goal of acute care is to enable access to the Line of Fine and no further. Understanding the role of various segments of healthcare is critical to understanding how you will reach patients and align your service with their desired outcomes.

In healthcare, the bookends of acute care are prevention and chronic management of a condition. In either of these phases, health consumers who are looking for options are less focussed on accessing rapid care and more interested in finding the best person or team for the job. When it comes to the bookends of healthcare, patients are looking for more nuanced advice, and practitioners should be prepared to offer it. Past the 'Line of Fine' the path to health is predicated, first and foremost, with where the patient/client/health consumer is at with respect to their interest, knowledge and prioritization of health. In short, their state of readiness. Once this is acknowledged, practitioners have the ability to deploy information and programming (an offer) that is aligned with where the patient currently stands with their health, with their nutritional and exercise choices and even their genetics.

Traditional medicine puts out fires. Their phone is always ringing. Their service offering is different from ours. If we want to truly serve the people whose lives we wish to impact, we cannot model our delivery of care after a system that serves its customers in a different way. Firefighters put out the flames; they do not rebuild the house. We need to design a model of care that inspires people to *want* to come to us, not feel forced to. When you deploy a model of care that matches where people are at in their lives, the model itself has the potential to become part of the medicine.

In Part Three, we will explore various models of care and health education that you can create and offer as a practitioner. But deciding on what you will build as a clinician entrepreneur first requires that you understand the journey of a health consumer and what informs their decision-making when it comes to investing time and energy into their health.

Serving your clients strategically requires attention and thought in four specific areas as a practitioner and, more importantly, as a clinician entrepreneur: (1) acknowledging the health consumer journey beyond one-to-one care; (2) moving from transactional to transformational care delivery; (3) identifying a clear niche or area of market authority; and (4) understanding the highest-value role you should be playing as a clinician with your patients.

First, understanding the journey and growth of a health consumer is critical to your success as a clinician entrepreneur. To help you understand this journey and the offerings you should and should not provide at each stage, I have devised a system called the Quadrants of Care. The Quadrants of Care are a framework that explains the state of readiness and the types of time, financial and emotional investments that health consumers will be willing to make at each leg of their health journey.

Second, the concept of transformation versus transaction is an important evolution from the pathogenic or traditional model of care. The idea that a series of transactions between practitioner and patient are the best way to achieve sustainable outcomes needs to be adjusted. Furthermore, when we acknowledge that someone's health is actually a function of the biopsychosocial interface of their biological, social and psychological environments, we have the potential to create a system and methodology of healing that honours the integration of factors that informs access to health or disease. Once again, the model of care itself becomes part of the medicine, and we move past the need to sell and convince patients on the idea of coming back, again and again, for regular follow-up visits.

Third is to create an arena of expertise for you and, potentially, your practice. When the house is on fire, we'll take anyone. When we are preventing the flames or rebuilding our home, we want the best person for the job. We are no longer in an era of practice development and clinical entrepreneurship that will spare those who are unwilling to be specific with their focus and expertise. I know the idea of 'choosing' a niche can be daunting or downright triggering for some. Coming up, we will discuss how you can 'have your cake and eat it too' when it comes to creating clarity about who you help.

Fourth, we will look at the three roles of a clinician—three types of 'hats' that any clinician wears. Knowing what hat to wear is what will enable you to build leverage in your business and will enable you to make the best use of your time. (Spoiler Alert: there's really only one hat that you *should* be wearing.)

CHAPTER 9

WHO ARE YOU HELPING?

love pizza. Gluten-free, gooey and with all of the toppings. What about you? What's your favourite indulgence? And when you do indulge, where do you go?

If I am going to indulge in gluten-free pizza, I am not heading to the catch-all fast-food joint that serves a side of sushi, gyros and fries. If I am going for pizza, I'm heading for that one place that makes pizza so good you'd swear you were sitting in a Roman trattoria, sipping wine and chowing down on a slice of thin-crust, marinara and mozzarella heaven. It's the same when you crave sushi: you don't go to your favourite Mexican restaurant that offers sushi on the side. Not when there's an amazing Japanese restaurant that specializes in the freshest nigiri, maki and sashimi.

With the advent of rapid search tools and the accessibility of 'virtual everything', consumers have transitioned from shopping for the closest thing to looking for the best in class. We look for the best place, product and person for the job at hand, whether it's pizza, or sushi, or even deodorant. We want the best plumber too—the professional one, not the roofer who fixes toilets on the side. In a word, we are 'picky'. We're selective. And if we're that judicious about pizza, sushi, deodorant and plumbers, you better believe we have serious preferences when it comes to our health. This was true BC, or 'before Covid'. It's even more true in the AC, 'after Covid' era of care delivery.

Pre-pandemic searches saw people using their computers to find the most convenient person, place or product that also happened to have a high rating. In healthcare, a large percentage of prospective health consumers were searching for a practitioner not based solely on their reputation or expertise, but by how close they were to work or home. The BC era still favoured, slightly, proximity searches with a secondary interest in landing on the best person for the job. Consumers looked at maybe five clinics within a certain proximity and then refined even further to make a selection based on the nicest website or cutest storefront. Surely a good clinician could be found in a place that looked like that—they'd book an appointment.

People shopped differently before COVID-19, so marketing was different to match. When the pandemic hit and people were stuck at home, they had time to take a closer look at what they were buying. And they took that time to click through websites and see exactly what they were getting for their money. People's priorities, standards and paradigms were changing. This was already true for some, but the pandemic put the rest over the edge.

People really came to understand and experience that they could do a lot online that they previously believed they had to do in person. COVID-19 simultaneously shifted their shopping methods and their beliefs around how care could be delivered. They didn't have to choose the pizza place on the corner—they could go to Italy. For practitioners, this meant that marketing had to change. They could no longer settle for being the generalist closest to a person's neighbourhood or office—they had to make themselves stand out as the best pizza, sushi, deodorant or plumber for the job. They had to find their niche; the group of people they were committed to serving.

You may have gotten away with not having a niche, BC, but you really stand to benefit from having one now, AC. You need clarity in terms of who you are helping and where you will establish authority in the market.

If you lack clarity around your audience or market—who you are helping first and foremost, your ideal, target patient—your marketing (and clinical efforts) lack clarity. When your marketing lacks clarity, you convey a lack of confidence. Trying to be everything to everyone isn't just confusing for the patient—it's expensive too. It takes more of your time and effort, and the marketing costs more too. People are no longer looking to find their condition listed on your website. They want more assurance that you can handle what they need. People don't feel included when you can treat acne *and* auto-immune conditions at the same time; they feel confused.

There are rare circumstances where generalizations work. For most, we remain open to everyone because we are scared to lay down roots and potentially say no to new business. We are worried about being pigeon-holed clinically or getting stuck treating only one thing. Generalizing brings negative consequences for your practice. It may seem counterintuitive, but niching down with as much clarity as possible will drive superior results.

WHY YOU MUST DEFINE AND
TARGET A NICHE

So we're clear on definitions, a niche (pronounced 'neesh') is a segment of a larger market that can be defined by its own unique needs, preferences or identity. For practitioners, this often means the confluence of the unique population you serve, the problem you solve, and the unique way you solve it. No generalization there. This typically means addressing a particular cluster of conditions or stage in someone's health, peri-natal care for example, or it can equally mean choosing to work with a fanatical group—a group of people so passionate that they seek specialized authorities to support their needs and understand their unique vantage. In my case, my niche, or what I have come to call my 'Arena of Authority', was working with entrepreneurs.

The idea of a niche is loaded with baggage. It is the concept we love to hate. So, let's think about it differently. A niche is not a narrow, limiting selection of the population—it is a decision to become a trusted authority. Trust is not built when you attempt to be everything to everyone. In what way and by whom do you want to be the trusted guide?

For those of you still stuck, one of the immediate kickbacks I hear around establishing a clinical focus is driven by the 'yeah, but' side of a clinician's brain—the side that is constantly hedging for opportunities. 'I'm a new practitioner, and I want to have all the experiences of treating every condition'. Or it laments, 'I'm worried that if I pick a niche, I'll never be able to treat anyone or any health issues outside my focus'.

I hear you, yet here's the thing... Instead of focussing on hypothetical downsides, consider the longer-term upside. For just a second, consider authority-building as a hole in the ground— a hole of opportunity. You're holding an umbrella of patients. Open the umbrella wide, and try jumping into the hole. See how you get stuck at the surface? Casting a wide net is keeping you from going deep. Now take most of those patients out of the umbrella, and leave only those, for now, most aligned with your clinical enthusiasm and authority. Now, with less drag, close the umbrella, and try jumping in that hole again, umbrella tip first. See how far down you could go? This is what happens when you work within your authority—you stop limiting yourself at the edges of opportunity, allow yourself to gain momentum and move even deeper in your career. And once you go deep, you have room to open that umbrella once again. It is not that you can't treat a variety of people—it's that you cannot start that way.

OPTION A — TRYING TO GO TOO WIDE TOO SOON

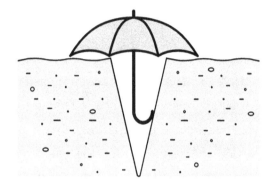

Figure 5a: The umbrella of short-lived opportunity.

OPTION B — GO DEEP AND THEN WIDE

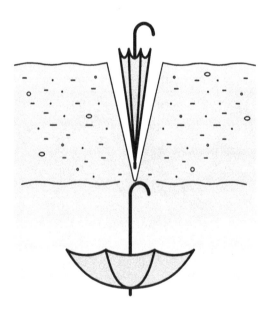

Figure 5b: The umbrella of deep sustainable opportunity.

Dr. Terry Wahls, a well-known, traditionally trained physician in the US, was diagnosed with multiple sclerosis. Terry wasn't satisfied with the idea of being on medication for the rest of her life or the rapid deterioration of her health. Seeking answers, she discovered and leaned into Functional Medicine. Applying the principles, she changed how she ate, adopted a paleo diet, and eventually, forced her disease into remission. She moved from being bound by a wheelchair to walking and accelerating at her career.

Terry taught her patients the principles of her treatment, going deep with her umbrella. Then, she did what most good clinicians do: she looked for a lateral connection to other autoimmune conditions that might benefit from her treatment. Because she dove down and established her roots, Dr. Wahls was able to open her umbrella and catch more opportunity. The Wahls Protocol went from being an approach that principally served patients with MS, to an accessible approach to a myriad of autoimmune conditions and a wider market. Dr. Wahls's authority and expertise lent itself to a natural expansion of her work, widening her Arena of Authority and applying her solution to a larger market. To reach more people over the long term and in a sustainable way, you must go narrow and deep before you cast a wider net.

Go deep, establish roots, and then open your umbrella. If you try it the other way around, you limit yourself and burn through the resources (time, energy, money and credibility) that you need to make the impact you're capable of, and that you desire.

FORGET NICHE—AIM FOR AN ARENA OF AUTHORITY

For many practitioners who hear the word niche, 'yeah, but' thoughts flood their heads: *I need all the patients I can get, so I'm not turning any of them away. Selecting a niche won't work for my business. I treat unique people…*

But do you?

We've all been there, and I totally get it, especially if you're a new clinician trying to establish your business and understand more about how you want to practice. Building authority in a narrow vertical seems 100 per cent counterintuitive to growing, and the last thing you want to do this early in your career is limit how many patients you accept. Other practitioners shy away from focussing because they're afraid they won't get the clinical confidence that comes from seeing a variety of patients and conditions. Here's the thing: whatever focus you lean into, it is not a decision set in stone. You can change it. Expand it. Narrow it. You can and likely will adapt the types of people you work with and the treatments you provide over time. This is exactly how it worked for me.

When I began my practice, I had the same worries. I was afraid to limit myself, the conditions I treated and the treatments I provided. I was afraid to focus on a specific group of health consumers. I was confident in my ability to provide a number of treatments for many conditions to all kinds of people, so why limit myself? But I realized that even though I could do all of those things, I had preferences. I most enjoyed working with patients who were willing to make a serious investment in their ongoing health. But who were these people? For a while, I thought I would focus on fertility, and then I seriously considered leaning into treating cancer. I had a proclivity towards supporting digestive health but kept getting into trouble from prominent referral sources when I would speak out about the connection between diet and symptoms. I could treat a variety of conditions, but strategically leaning into everything was burning me out and leaving me nowhere.

Resolving my challenge would not come down to thinking about the problem like everyone else. I too was equipped and wanted to work with a variety of people, but I was unwavering in my desire to support people passionate about making an investment in their health. One day, while pitching a business as part of an entrepreneurial event, I found myself face-to-face with my clinical future. As my team and I passionately and energetically presented our idea, I realized I had a noticeable and unfair advantage over my competition—I was genuinely healthy. I wasn't jacked on my tenth cup of coffee or crawling across the finish line; I had the ultimate entrepreneurial advantage. My brain *and* my body had my back. I was healthier than most everyone else in the room. That was the moment I made my decision, and I never looked back. I chose to work with entrepreneurs.

These people were goal-oriented and disciplined. They were committed to success in their businesses and with their health. Their careers made special demands of them, and I could help them excel in the face of those requirements. Not only that, but I spoke their language. I understood why they stayed up late, the language of a term sheet, and the unrelenting desire to create a meaningful business.

I created my brand, Entrepology, with a mission of giving entrepreneurs an unfair advantage in the marketplace by making their brains and bodies available to them at a moment's notice. I was having my cake and eating it too. I was able to treat a variety of people and health concerns, but I marketed towards and spoke to a unique vertical of the population. Once I made the decision, my practice exploded. People knew how to refer to me. I became the go-to practitioner for entrepreneurs, treating some of the most prominent entrepreneurs and business people in the country.

This experience made me realize that there was a second type of niche: supporting a fanatical group.

A fanatical group is a cluster of people who are passionately living their purpose. They may be entrepreneurs, vegans, cyclists or gamers. The obsession is less important than the feature—their health is a means to excel at their craft.

Choosing a fanatical group enables you to keep the conditions you treat varied. It almost guarantees that you get to work with a motivated audience, and it checks all of the traditional boxes of selecting a niche. You're welcome.

There will always be limiting beliefs around niching. Practitioners may lament that they live in a small town and the market just isn't big enough or that their Arena of Authority of choice is too narrow to attract enough patients. Those objections used to make sense, before technology changed our ability to reach more people in more places. The added bonus is that being among the best at that particular thing that you do, for those particular health needs, shared by a particular group of people, allows you to charge a higher premium. In so many ways and for so many reasons, establishing authority always outweighs a generalized approach.

FINDING YOUR AUTHORITY

Finding your Arena of Authority isn't as difficult as it seems, even if you are currently treating a wide variety of conditions. Start by asking yourself, 'Who do I want to help?'

As a reminder, the whole first part of this book was about *intention*, the first letter in IMPACT. Be intentional in selecting your authority: *know what you want and why you want it.*

Consider these three options to help guide you to your authority acquisition:

Core medical problem or condition: Identify a condition that you can treat well and enjoy addressing in practice. This is not too narrow by any means. For example, think of all the women who suffer from osteoporosis, yet so few practitioners specialize in the prevention and treatment of this condition.

Methodology of treatment: If you have a methodology for approaching a condition or treating a cluster of conditions, you may have a niche. Consider the many therapies available that require specialized equipment, knowledge and experience. Designing a unique approach with discernable outcomes is another path towards authority. Think about the groups of people who would most benefit from your approach. Direct your energy towards the largest group and expand as you gain traction. (We'll delve deeper into designing your methodology soon.)

Fanatical group: As an entrepreneur myself, I was able to connect with this 'fanatical', irrationally passionate group of fellow entrepreneurs. You may want to zero in on people with whom you share interests or who are in careers in which you're familiar. Is your partner in finance? You may have insight into the ailments common with people in that industry. Do you have children involved in sports, or do you love to run? You may know more than you think about people who run marathons, their health conditions and their desired health statuses and outcomes. This is a perfect approach if you want to ensure maximized exposure to a variety of conditions.

Get a notepad or open a file, and start jotting down some ideas around the types of patients you'd like to treat. Start with a list of conditions. Add your preferred treatments. Look for commonalities between the two groups. This is where you start to focus. You can narrow your market even further by selecting a fanatical group that suffers from that common condition or conditions, or who seek a shared outcome, and who are amenable to the treatment or treatments you provide.

You can work backwards too, beginning with the people. Say you prefer treating women. That's a huge market. Narrow it by choosing to treat women with osteoporosis. Finally, you may have a certain methodology for treating women with osteoporosis. And if you don't, don't worry; we'll get there.

There is one requirement in selecting a target market that traditionally remains unsaid, and it is with consideration for your access to momentum that I will address it. *You must acknowledge that in running a healthcare practice outside of an acute setting, your patient population must be able and willing to invest in your services.* There are stages of life where the decision to invest in one's health becomes a more proximate priority.

A woman I'll call 'April' was active in one of our programmes. She had a huge passion for assisting women in their breastfeeding journey. April created programming and education material to help women feel empowered during a lonely and challenging part of their post-partum journey. As a mother and practitioner, she was adamant that the best time for a mother to gain support and education around breastfeeding was *before* they gave birth. She was likely correct. The challenge for April was that she was viewing the problem solely from the lens of the practitioner. Delving deeper into the psychology and life stage of April's avatar would have revealed a group of young women excited to invest in their babies—that is, their babies' nurseries, strollers and adorable little onesies. They did not feel the pressure or have the desire to invest in their breastfeeding journey before they even had the baby in hand. Breastfeeding was not a problem they needed solved.

There will be times, as you understand your avatar on a deeper level, where you will be forced to acknowledge the discrepancy between what you want for your clients and what they are looking for. They have to *want* to make the investment, do the work and open themselves up to you. Know your audience well enough to be able to make the distinction.

Once you've identified those people you want to help, go deep. Really deep. Come up with a character who exemplifies your Arena of Authority. Give her a name, an age and a personal health challenge. Then go deeper, explore her psychographics—the psychological and sociological factors that inform her decisions. Get to know her deepest fears and desires, like you were about to play her character in a movie. Get clear on the ways that you can help deliver the outcome *she* is looking to achieve. As you develop your practice, look to this character, your avatar, to guide your authority-driven business and treatment decisions. Understanding your prospective health consumers at this level is the most respectful work you can do as you design a roadmap to support their health.

THE OPTION TO BRANCH OUT

Your avatar represents the feelings, decision-making metrics and values of your primary market. As you step into your authority, your one to two avatars will become the audience you write to, speak to and design solutions for. Most of your patients are going to be similar to this imaginary person you've created, within a range. They may be aged forty-five to fifty-five, and they may be working professionals in a certain industry, or across several industries, or they may be marathon runners. Who they are is the number-one focus of your work. Your advertising, marketing, treatments, methodologies and everything else is tailored to attract and, just as importantly, honour the needs of these people. The better you know them, the more credible you will become, and the more willing they will be to trust you with their health.

That does not mean you will always treat just this market. You can branch out. You might discover other conditions that are common among a number of your patients, or you may find yourself saying yes to their partners and kids. You may even find a secondary fanatical group that benefits from your offerings. You can do anything you want, as long as you remember to be intentional about it and judicious in your assessment and evaluation of whether or not it is working. Decide whether you want to expand or stay narrow and consider the effects of that choice. It's all up to you and what you want for your practice and your life.

CHECK-IN

1. If I asked my friends to select a niche or an Arena of Authority for me, what would they say? Do I resonate with their selection?
2. Who or what do I not want to be treating? (Hint: then stop.)
3. Do I have a story or connection to a particular type of patient?
4. When I look at my schedule, who are the people I am excited to work with? What do they have in common?
5. Why do I do the work I do? What is my 'why'? Who will resonate with this idea?
6. In getting to know my ideal client, what gets them out of bed in their own life? In other words, why do they need their health?
7. Can my ideal client afford to work with me?
8. If my ideal client were to spend their money on something else, what would it be and why?

9. What is the common World View I share with my client? (E.g. Do I share a love of children, dogs or video games, or perhaps do we all believe that everyone deserves better health?)

CHAPTER 10

THE BIGGEST OPPORTUNITY OF YOUR CAREER

The Quadrants of Care

The relationship between patient and practitioner has been one-to-one for as long as medicine has been practiced. This relationship is considered the norm and gold standard of care delivery, even though it may not be optimal for either party in many situations. We have predicated our model of practice on two significant assumptions; first, that traditional one-to-one care delivery is the best way to work with patients and, secondly, that this is what people want. But what if we are wrong? What if the model we need to build health is different from the model we currently deploy to manage disease? And if so, when will we make that change?

When I set out to grow my business, I attended a lot of meetings and conferences, trying to expose myself to as many novel approaches and ideas as possible. One piece of advice that came up over and over again was to get in front of more people and talk—basically, do more to establish my credibility. I welcomed this advice. Public speaking was a skill in which I excelled: speaking, sometimes to exhaustion, was something that fueled me (I know I am lucky in this department). This was especially true when I had the opportunity to speak on something that excited me, like health.

I set out to find speaking engagements that aligned with my practice and quickly landed an opportunity where I would talk about gut health to a roomful of roughly sixty-five people suffering from inflammatory bowel disease. I had treated many patients for Crohn's disease and colitis, so I had much to share with the audience. The talk went well, and I could feel the energy in the room—so much so, that I invited everyone in attendance to visit me in my office. These were potential patients, and they seemed genuinely interested in everything I had to say on a topic that affected their health.

Of the sixty-five enthusiastic people in the audience, just three took me up on my offer. This wasn't a boring talk to a bunch of uninterested people. I nailed it. They showed up specifically to hear me talk about gut health. They were a lively, engaged audience. Why weren't they interested in pursuing a solution to what ailed them?

Curious, I queried the patients who did show up, and I asked others who came to see me later for gut health and other health issues—especially those patients who had been suffering for a while.

I wanted to know what prevented them from seeking my help sooner, and the answers surprised me. People were afraid I would tell them to stop drinking coffee or to adjust their diet. They were afraid I'd pry into their medical history, and they didn't want to share certain details, intimate details such as abortions or their use of drugs. Rarely would the cost of care be the cause of their delay. They weren't ready for care that required this level of vulnerability.

Though their answers varied widely, they all shared a common thread: these people were afraid of the *emotional* risk that accompanied an in-depth, one-to-one interaction. Not just with me, but with any clinician. The relationship risked putting them in a very vulnerable position, and they weren't ready for it. Being asked to tell their secrets, change their habits, or come up with more money than they wanted to pay felt confrontational. They delayed treatment and allowed the progression of their disease or potential health because the one-to-one offer was wrong for them.

That is on us. The way to help more health consumers, I learned, was to create opportunities that mitigated vulnerability and feelings of confrontation. The new goal was to ensure that I had more than one means to reach people who were interested in transforming their health. I wanted to give them control over the relationship, instead of being the authority in a one-to-one encounter who asked all the questions, gave all the marching orders and expected to be paid for my time.

Figure 6: The Quadrants of Care represent the patient journey and the possible mechanics of care that match their state of readiness.

THE QUADRANTS OF CARE

That singular realization put me on a path of Discovery. I wanted to understand patients' health journeys outside of their interactions with me. How were they managing their health, and what did I need to change about how I delivered healthcare to better serve them? Instead of inviting them in for an appointment, I had to meet health consumers where they were. I organized my findings into four Quadrants of Care: Aspirational, Empowerment, Strategy and Growth. Figure 6 illustrates these Quadrants: what they are from the patient's perspective and your role in each quadrant.

Figure 7: The Quadrants of Care with corresponding examples of offerings.

The Aspirational Quadrant

The first Quadrant of Care, the Aspirational Stage of a person's health journey, is the *aha* moment when they realize that health is accessible through their own actions. This is not to say that practitioners do not have a role, but for those on a journey past the Line of Fine, the Aspiration Stage/Quadrant is where they acquire a vocabulary and a set of options for their health. Before they realized the power of this stage, health consumers outsourced their health through visits with a practitioner, prescriptions and the wonders of pharmacology.

For a health consumer in the Aspirational Quadrant, the person has become aware and enlightened—someone or something has opened their eyes to the fact that they can take control of their health. Today, that wake-up call often comes from people's cell phones in the form of social media, podcasts and online articles. When a patient learns about a potentially life-altering action that can positively impact their health, and they opt in to try it, they effectively take control. The actions may be as simple as switching from coffee to herbal tea to avoid caffeine jitters. It may be a natural remedy for controlling their menstrual cycle or a change in diet that impacts their previously normalized constipation. This quadrant is an opportunity to disseminate health without the financial or vulnerability burden of a one-to-one visit, and most importantly, it enables health consumers to *experience* the effects of positive, simple changes in their health and sense of well-being.

As a personal example, when I decided that Lupron was not right for me, I was out of 'traditional' options. I turned to the internet for answers. I changed my diet, cut out dairy and started on some basic, self-prescribed supplementation. For the first time in over twenty-four months, I felt better. The more I learned, the deeper I wanted to go in driving my own health and healing.

You can provide value to patients in this quadrant with your own content. You may not be able to—or even want to—monetise the transaction in this quadrant, but in exchange for the content, you can request something more valuable: the person's email address.

When you share compelling, accessible information with people that actually moves the needle for them, they begin to look to you as a trusted authority on their health. This is your opportunity to satisfy the intention that drove you towards this system of care in the first place—'doctor' literally means 'teacher'—and this is where you get to shine.

As a clinician with a million years (modest exaggeration) of school behind you, you are awash with the information that health consumers are seeking. The Aspirational Quadrant is your opportunity to share *what* you know. This is not the place to deliver dosing or strategy—the real value you have to sell to health consumers. Rather, this is the place that should inspire health consumers to get started. Leveraging the Aspirational Stage of a patient's journey requires that you know *who* you are speaking to and *what* they will need to get started and inspired. You will not engender trust or a following in this stage attempting to be everything to everyone, but with discipline and clarity, you will affect people's lives. You might not relish the idea of starting a podcast, getting on video or committing to social media, but recognize that it is a critical entry point for eager and committed health consumers. There are lots of options available to you in this quadrant. As you gain traction and success, you can outsource the creation of this essential content. Your credentials may accelerate the trust factor with health consumers, but credentials alone do not replace the need to build the 'know, like and trust' factor with prospective patients. Regardless of your professional designation, people require multiple contact points with you before they typically pull the trigger to commit or purchase. Avoiding the creation of content in this quadrant makes your job more difficult.

I know this is the source of some resistance. I know, for many of you, creating content will push you outside of your comfort zone. But remember, 'doctor' means 'teacher', and avoiding this calling means leaving a lot of potential health consumers—and future revenue—on the table.

The Empowerment Quadrant (a.k.a. the DIY Quadrant)

People who hang out in the Aspirational Quadrant eventually become more comfortable and confident with the idea of controlling and investing in their health. With that sense of control comes a migration to the second stage of the consumer health journey: the Empowerment Quadrant, also known as the DIY (do-it-yourself) Quadrant. In this stage, health consumers begin investing in their health beyond the free information and 'inspiration' on Instagram. They might pay for advanced guidance, such as a book, yoga class or online course about their condition or goal. Whatever they do in this stage, the differentiating factor is their willingness to invest in the deeper journey of their health.

For the practitioner, this quadrant can be frustrating. People in the Empowerment Quadrant tend to follow a somewhat chaotic path to health. One month, they're on a juice cleanse, and the next month, they're on a keto diet. They might get their content from a variety of sources, and it isn't always congruent. Whatever people choose to do in the Empowerment Quadrant, you as a clinician have to take a deep breath, relax and roll with it. The person will not take kindly to your pointing out whether whatever they're doing is actually helping. The stage of self-exploration and control is critical for deeper, committed engagement in the future.

Despite often watching in frustration, you will however find opportunity in this unstructured stage of health exploration. People's newfound interest in their health, their eagerness to take control of it and their willingness to pay for guidance will be given to those 'influencers' in the Aspirational Stage who provided health consumers with the most confidence and clarity about the journey ahead. If you've written a book or created an online course, leverage that content and your authority to engage with people, or lead them through a tool like an online course, in the Empowerment Quadrant. Providing support in this phase does not mean you don't need to take them on officially as a patient, schedule visits or meet with them one-to-one. Your role in this stage will be to provide information, not strategy. Ideally, you will provide content that moves them closer to the starting point of your care.

In this quadrant, you can begin to layer and leverage your content and teachings. Any content you provide to people who have entered the Empowerment Quadrant on their own can also be made available to your in-office patients. The content and programming in the Empowerment or DIY Quadrant are the things you wish your avatar knew, implemented and commanded *before* they became your patient. This quadrant is an opportunity to prepare your ideal clients for what comes next and to provide access to strategic information at a fraction of the price and redundancy that would be required for you to teach it in a one-to-one appointment. This stage is where you have the opportunity to reach more people through innovation (book, course or even a Peloton), reserving the one-to-one phase for the delivery of your most strategic care.

The Strategy Quadrant

The journey towards health is not linear. The use of quadrants to describe the journey of a health consumer is an intentional acknowledgement of the unique determinants of health that inform each health consumer's journey. People won't always go from the first quadrant to the second and then on to the third.

The Strategy Stage of care is what you were trained to provide. This is where the one-to-one visit resides, and this is where people come, not for more *information*, but for a *transformation*. This is where we individualize the care and sell our most valuable asset as clinicians, our strategy. People who migrate to the Strategy Quadrant typically do so because they know they need immediate support, are seeking a deeper experience or have yet to achieve the outcome they are seeking. They are willing to invest emotionally, practically and financially for a customised transformation. They may have invested in a course or tried a new diet or lifestyle change, but they did not get all the results they wanted. They feel as if they're part way there, but they still need more. They aren't ready to abandon their content source, though, because the information has been exceptional and beneficial. They may have witnessed other people getting more dramatic results with the same guidance, and they're thinking they need extra help to get there. With the exception of enthused referrals and recommendations from friends (influencers in their private lives), the Strategy Quadrant is rarely someone's first stop. With this context and an understanding of the other Quadrants of Care, you can see why building a practice with only a Strategy Quadrant offering is slow to gain momentum and reinforces the fear of early-stage practitioners that they need to be saying yes to every patient who walks through their door.

The transformational experience that characterizes the Strategic Quadrant is something we will tackle in greater detail in Chapter 11.

The Growth Quadrant

When I was in school studying Naturopathic Medicine, we talked a lot about how to maintain contact and engagement with our patients when they 'finished care'. The general consensus was that 'enticing' patients to come back once they had achieved their desired outcome was unethical or gimmicky. Some suggested that you could book them in for an annual physical exam but agreed that patients should return when they see fit. As a new grad, eager to follow an ethical and proven approach to care, I used the same framework in my practice. I advised checking in if something came up, and I suggested that they return for their annual physical exam. I then released them to thrive in their new state of optimized health.

Only they didn't thrive. Many floundered. Heading back to the same family, stress, job, grocery store, stories, beliefs and life meant that they quickly slipped into their old way of health. Like clockwork, my patients didn't return for their physicals; they returned with their original symptoms eighteen to twenty-four months after we initially solved their problem. My own health journey didn't stop once I got my symptoms under control; it has been a lifelong commitment. While the intensity and frequency of the interventions changed, the need for support, accountability, inspiration and *growth* remained. Our patients are no different. It is not unethical to design a continuity phase to your clinical ecosystem; it is unethical *not* to. This is the role of the Growth Quadrant: to support health consumers or your patients in their ongoing commitment towards living a healthier life.

There are two ways that patients or health consumers enter the Growth Quadrant. The first is by patients whose experiences and outcomes in the Empowerment (DIY) Quadrant have exceeded their expectations. These individuals often skip the Strategy Quadrant altogether. They don't need to see you or access your strategic care. These health consumers head straight to the Growth Quadrant. They achieved their desired outcome (on their own), and now they want to lean deeper into their health. Let them. They followed your guidance outside of the one-to-one model, and they're satisfied or even elated with the results. Because they progressed at *their* pace, on *their* time, knowing up front the investment of time and cost *and* without having to disclose their deepest darkest secrets, they are happily ready to go deeper.

The Growth Quadrant is also a natural next phase for your one-to-one clients who achieved their result. They no longer need you in a traditional one-to-one context, but they aren't equipped to maintain all of their changes or perhaps even achieve more without additional guidance.

In my own practice, the Growth Phase included access to an ongoing membership with online webinars, an in-person speaker series and a discount on their supplements. I could have made it more complicated, but I didn't need to. I earned predictable recurring revenue each month, kept my patients engaged and furthered their health journey—all while keeping my schedule open for strategic clients who needed my personal attention and care.

EXPANDING BEYOND ONE-TO-ONE CARE

Many practitioners claim that one-to-one care works fine for them, and they don't see a reason to change. That may be true, for now, but what happens when you are tired, want a vacation, have a baby or need time away to care for ageing parents? Are you able to put your income and momentum on hold? Do you want the pressure of being dependent on a single income stream, tied exclusively to you? One-to-one care is expensive to deliver. It's a high-risk proposition for the patient, taking an undetermined amount of time out of their day and money from their wallet. It is more than what most people need to set them on a road to health. It takes away much of their power and renders their outcomes heavily dependent on you. The one-to-one model of healthcare is built on two massive assumptions: that people want it and that it's the best way to deliver optimized health.

While one-to-one care is important, it is expensive and extremely risky financially to deploy as your sole source of income. Furthermore, it is not a model that is amenable to all health consumers. We've over-indexed the importance of one-to-one care, and we have rarely questioned the model. Until now.

The Quadrants of Care and the opportunities they provide create better long-term outcomes and more financially sustainable healthcare. They meet patients where *they* are. It enables health consumers to become more engaged in their health journey, seeking you and your strategy when they are ready. This makes it easier for you both.

The benefits to the practitioner are so obvious, it's hard to imagine not wanting to diversify offers adjacent to your one-to-one practice. It is a 'cake and eat it too' model.

Giving yourself and your customers options is the ultimate 'boss move' as an entrepreneur. For me, I am never thinking exclusively about how a business will make me more money, but I am *always* looking to see how it will provide me with more options. That is the promise I have made to my future self. Ironically, it is the reason I chose to practice Naturopathic Medicine; I wanted my patients and other women like me to have more options in their life and health.

CHECK-IN

1. What are the ways patients or health consumers can currently learn or access care from my business?

2. What would change in my one-to-one practice if the content or information was packaged to be reviewed outside of my office, such as an online training portal?

3. Brainstorming with the Quadrants of Care, what types of offerings could I consider including to move patients forward beyond one-to-one practice?

CHAPTER 11

TRANSFORMATION VS. TRANSACTION

The traditional, transactional healthcare process relies on charging patients for access to your time and expertise. Transformational healthcare, by contrast, begins with a goal in mind: to take the patient from their current state of health and paradigm of where you provide treatments for their conditions and occasions to a desired outcome (more on this in a second), *and* to maintain or even continuously improve that health over the long term. Transformational healthcare is a journey facilitated by you over a set amount of time for the benefit of your patient. The patient doesn't just call for an appointment when they're sick or injured—they take an active role in their own health, with you as their guide.

When my mom turned seventy, I gave her a trip to Italy. She was overwhelmed. This was her bucket-list trip. We only had fourteen days, and she had an aggressive list of places she wanted to visit. Pulling the pieces together was not simply about knocking the places off the list; she wanted to *feel* Italy. This was not a travel-book kind of trip—I didn't have the time or knowledge to help her experience Italy the way she wanted, so I hired a guide. I worked with a travel consultant who lifted the veil on Italy for us. We had private cooking classes overlooking olive orchards in Tuscany and a private guided tour of the Sistine Chapel and were led to bookstores and artist studios known only to locals. We didn't just see Italy; we were transformed by the experience. Some types of travel are best suited for a DIY experience (hey, Florida) while others can facilitate a moment of complete transformation.

Most practitioners still treat their patients like a trip to Florida (I love Florida, by the way). 'You should visit Disney World, hit the beach and definitely sample the saltwater taffy'. They give them a list of 'shoulds', cautionary tales on inaction and ask them to check in once the trip is done. If a patient comes in with a urinary tract infection or a broken leg—a few quick transactions and the problem is solved. Unless, of course, this is the fourth UTI this year. Practitioners who address the 'root cause' of illness will recognize the opportunity to address the lifestyle, microbiome and nutrient status of a person managing chronic urinary tract infections, but to be effective, they must also recognize that few people will be able to implement and maintain the required changes without strategic support. Changing the foundation of someone's health does not happen through handouts, supplements or in-office treatments alone. It won't be adhered to if a patient is continuously told to 'book back in a few weeks, we'll see how it's going and take it from there'. *'If you enjoy Rome and the Colosseum, we'll talk about other Italian highlights on our next call and hopefully we can fit them in before you have to go back to your real life'.*

Health and healing are a journey; we all know that, yet we resist designing the experience of health beyond a simple map. In the absence of knowing where they are headed and the next goalpost in their healing work, people often abandon the trip. For us as clinicians, the lack of communication at the onset triggers an endless series of visits where we are forever forced to 'sell' the next step, endlessly hoping that people stick with us. We have the knowledge to build health, but we deploy a model that was designed to transact around the treatment of disease.

Transformational care outlines the journey before the patient gets on the plane. It manages expectations around potential changes, and it highlights the main features and anticipated outcomes (not promised) of the trip. Transformational care recognizes that people want to pack and plan appropriately. As the purveyor of this care, with experience in a given country, it becomes your responsibility to note the weather, the terrain and currency required for the journey. When you manage these expectations, it instils confidence in your traveller, and it informs them on how to pack.

For those working on the other side of the Line of Fine, the Transformational Model is the best approach for delivering growth and health over the long term.

THREE PHASES OF CARE

Delivering care through transformation recognizes that there are three phases to the clinician–client relationship and care: Discovery, Action and Growth.

Discovery Phase of Care

When addressing the root cause of illness or chronic pain, or simply working to optimize one's state of health, gathering a comprehensive understanding of the biopsychosocial elements of one's life are critical. For most of our patients, this frequently amounts to 'the most comprehensive and in-depth' medical intake of someone's life. While valuable for some, this is an incredibly vulnerable phase for others and must be treated with respect. The Discovery Phase is also a self-contained stage of someone's care that includes the interview and 'disclosure' of the comprehensive plan and clinician's perspective and assessment of the problem.

The Discovery Phase is usually comprised of two appointments. The first is a typical intake in which you complete a comprehensive evaluation and interview of the new client/patient to assess and assimilate their health status.

The second appointment/touchpoint is introduced to walk the patient through a comprehensive roadmap of their care, set expectations, provide a report of findings and, most importantly, create buy-in for the upcoming process. This appointment could be virtual or in-person. It could include treatment or not. The nuance of the experience rests in the hands of the practitioner. Most critical, however, are the series of appointments that will assure them of the best ongoing care for their condition, illness, injury or desired outcome. The patient, at this point, will feel more empowered because you are inviting them into their own health plan. They see the value and their ability to opt in or out, for better or for worse. Not all patients will opt in, but if you want to work with people who have an active, ongoing interest in their health, this process will help you define that audience.

How you charge for a transformational package or experience depends on the regulations in your jurisdiction (state, province or country). You may be able to charge all at once or over several billing periods. The details of how you collect the payment become less important when you lead with the discussion of a transformational experience. Convey the options for how you will move forward towards the end of the Discovery Phase, often in the second appointment and as you bridge the experience towards the Active Phase of care.

Active Phase of Care
(Where You Solve the Problem)

Once the Discovery Phase is complete and the patient has opted in to your transformational model, treatments and check-ins continue with open and regular conversations between the practitioner (possibly health coach) and the patient. Health consumers want your strategy, coaching and confidence as you lead them towards the solution you have played out for their health.

This is not as simple as it sounds, but it's where you have the opportunity to really move the needle with respect to the patient's health. You have to take the time to dig deeper into their overall health and their health goals. This isn't just about fixing a broken leg—it's about addressing the ingredients and physiological complexities that will inform optimal health for your patient. To get there, you have to acknowledgement and remedy the root of what is hindering that objective. This cannot, as you know, happen by addressing everything at once. The patient would be overwhelmed, and healing does not take place in this manner. Root-cause medicine, regardless of your training, means addressing health like layers of an onion, peeling back each section and supporting effective resolution or stabilization before moving on to the next. For this reason, the Active Phase of Care is broken down into a series of 'phases' strategically designed to support systematic healing. Each pillar includes baseline testing, along with defining desired outcomes and milestones to track along the way.

My practice focussed on entrepreneurs and high performers. While they cared about their health, for most, they were interested in how their health could be leveraged as a tool to optimize their business or quality of life. Recognizing the outcome they were after, I made a simple promise to my ideal client avatar: I will make your brain and body available to you at a moment's notice. Achieving this was not always possible, but it was a benchmark that I aimed towards. People who wanted weight loss or fertility support went somewhere else. To achieve the outcome of my ideal clients, I moved my patients through three distinct phases of Active care. I defined criteria of eligibility for the Active Phase of Care, and I attended to the unique needs of my patients before they moved through three distinct phases.

Phase 1 supported optimized digestive health. Key milestones were standardised and were aligned with specific functional testing. When I presented my patients with their care plan, I outlined their base digestive health status and where we wanted them to be. Some were close to the desired outcome, but many needed additional support. The length of each phase was predicated on the support they required. Their care plan outlined our respective responsibilities and an educated timeline to achieve the milestones for that phase of care. They didn't need to achieve perfect digestive health, but they had to hit a base standard.

Following digestive health, I repeated the process for hormones. This again included functional testing, desired milestones, and lifestyle support accompanied by strategic interventions from me. We both knew where we were heading and *why* a recommendation had been made. For some people, no intervention was needed. In these cases, I referred them to additional endocrine knowledge through online training, and we moved on to the final pillar of care.

Once digestion and hormonal health had been addressed, usually over four to six months, I moved on to supporting neurological and mitochondrial health. This was where I addressed energy and optimal brain support. Supporting the brain and body of an entrepreneur took time. While there was always individualization, most people required support in key strategic ways. It was always easier to manage the exception than to treat everyone like a fresh story.

Criteria of Eligibility

So, what happens when someone comes through the door who doesn't fit neatly into the box? When Mary (not her real name) came into my office, she was a mess. She had a binder full of problems, a full family life and a busy business. She desperately wanted her brain and body to work at the speed of her ambition. While I explained to Mary how my system worked, we both acknowledged that she was not ready. Her diet was a mess, she was concerned about her blood pressure and engaging in any type of exercise, and she flat out refused to try any type of supplementation. For my transformational process to work, Mary was going to have change her relationship with food, get her blood pressure under control and support her mindset around the benefits of self-care. For three months, she worked with me, our nutritionist and our mindset coach outside of the 'transformational experience' to get her ready to move into Active care.

Nine months later, Mary had lost twenty-five pounds, her blood pressure was under control, she exercised sort of regularly, and most importantly, her brain and body were available to her the way she had dreamt of. My process allowed for the exception instead of being defined by it. As a result, Mary achieved the result she was looking for and was ready for more. We were ready to move on from the Active Phase of Mary's Care and transition towards her ongoing state of health growth.

Growth Phase of Care

None of us are done with our health. It is not a destination that we reach and can then forget. And yet, that is exactly how our care system is designed. When I was a student, I was obsessed with understanding the nuance of how we communicated with patients. As my patients approached the phase where we had 'resolved' their problem, I was endlessly curious about how we spoke about ongoing care. To my surprise, most of my supervisors had little insight or strategy when it came to this phase of our practitioner–patient relationship. 'Invite them to return if something comes up', was one suggestion. 'Book them in for their annual Pap', suggested another. 'Above all, don't invent reasons to keep seeing them; it's unethical', was the universal consensus.

When 'Adam' came to see me for the first time, he was close to 370lbs. He knew something needed to change. This was early in my career, and I heeded the advice of my previous supervisors when it came to not over-extending care. I worked with Adam for nearly a year and eventually enabled him to reach his goal weight of 250lbs. He had a ways to go in terms of his health, but he was eager to stick to our plan on his own. With nothing left to offer (I thought), I invited him to check in twelve months later for an annual appointment. He obliged and was booked in a year in advance.

Adam called twice to move his annual check-in until finally, after nearly eighteen months, he returned to my office. When he finally came through my door, I was shocked. He had gained back all of the weight and more. When Adam had last left my office, he was eager and enthused to take his health into his own hands. We had both treated his achievement—losing 120lbs—like a destination. Once we had seen the sights and done the tour, there was no further need for a guide. Only this was not Rome. When Adam went back to his life without me, he went back to his stressors, his familiar grocery store patterns and family gatherings filled with messaging about food that had been decades in the making.

The Growth Phase of Care is about maintaining momentum, going deeper into one's healing and preventing patients like Adam from taking two steps forward and five steps back. It is also about providing this support in a manner that is economical for patients and less dependent on your time as a practitioner. Health consumers who opt in to the Growth Phase are entering an ongoing, longer-term process of health optimization and maintenance. The Growth Phase of Care recognizes that the moment when you achieve an outcome for a patient is the moment where you have their captive attention and trust. For some this might mean setting them free, but for many, it means that there is a tremendous opportunity to offer the patient access to ongoing growth, improvement and strategies for self-reliance.

Mechanistically, the Growth Phase of Care offerings can often become the most creative. In my practice, patients were invited to join a monthly membership that afforded them access to special events, a speaker series and discounts from strategic partners. When people pay, they pay attention, and this model was a tool to remind people that they had made a commitment to prioritize their health. For other practitioners, the Growth Phase has become an opportunity to offer group programming or packaged access to a health coach. The options are endless.

The Growth Phase is perhaps the most severe departure from the traditional, transactional approach to healthcare. But unlike care delivered within the confines of the Line of Fine, health optimization knows no bounds, and neither can your system of healing.

PULLING IT ALL TOGETHER: THE ACTION FRAMEWORK

[THE A.C.T.I.O.N FRAMEWORK]

DEEPER CONSIDERATIONS

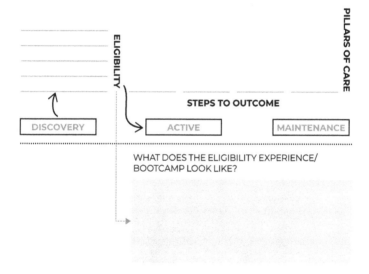

Figure 8: This is a roadmap of the complete ACTION framework, including pillars of care. A fillable PDF and supportive training are available at **impactmedicinebook.com/resources.**

In the last chapter, I introduced you to the Quadrants of Care: Aspirational, Empowerment, Strategy and Growth. It's important to understand how these quadrants interact with the Phases of Care. They fall within the Strategy Quadrant.

Delivering care in the Strategic Quadrant is a transformational experience and offering. The delivery in this quadrant can be simple or more hands-on. It could be deployed as a 'programme' or through a series of individual sessions that present as a transformation. The manner in which you deliver your transformational process will principally be determined by the regulations and programme limitations in the jurisdiction where you practice.

Knowing that you need to develop key Phases of Care is helpful, but what lies below these descriptions is critical to defining a successful process. For over six years and in working with over one thousand practitioners globally, I have defined a framework that outlines the most important considerations of a strategic care plan. It is known as the ACTION framework.

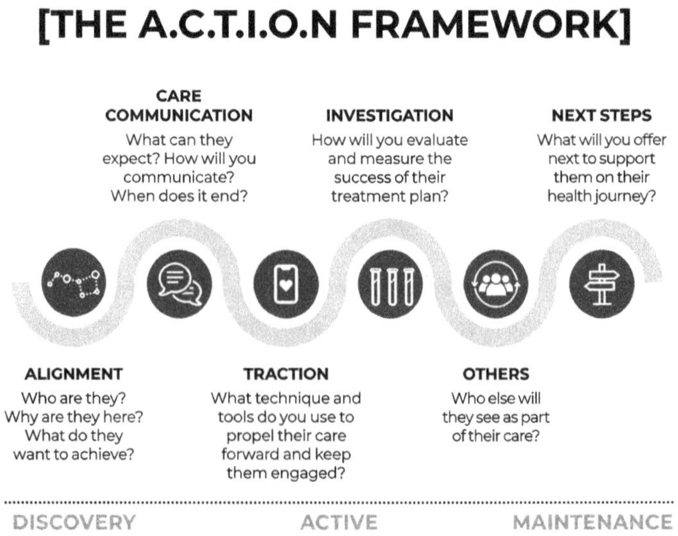

[THE A.C.T.I.O.N FRAMEWORK]

CARE COMMUNICATION
What can they expect? How will you communicate? When does it end?

INVESTIGATION
How will you evaluate and measure the success of their treatment plan?

NEXT STEPS
What will you offer next to support them on their health journey?

ALIGNMENT
Who are they? Why are they here? What do they want to achieve?

TRACTION
What technique and tools do you use to propel their care forward and keep them engaged?

OTHERS
Who else will they see as part of their care?

DISCOVERY · · · ACTIVE · · · MAINTENANCE

Figure 9: The ACTION Framework is a comprehensive overview of the transformational journey and the required components to deliver a transformational experience.

Alignment

The A in ACTION stands for alignment. Consider the alignment regarding your patients' demographics, psychographics and health statusographics—where they are with respect to their health. Also, ask yourself if the outcome they desire is one that you can deliver. In short, get clear on who you treat and what you deliver for them. Ensure that your patients match the niche you've identified for your practice and confirm that these are the people for whom you really want to provide care.

Communication and Care Strategy

Communication, the C in ACTION, is a critical ingredient for the establishment of trust and buy-in. Creating a tool and taking your patients through a roadmap of your process is not an optional step. It is crucial within a transformational process that your patients understand the path you've outlined for them and how you will work together to get them where they want to go. You can access examples of how to set up a Care Plan document at impactmedi cinebook.com/resources.

Traction

Traction is how you keep your patients moving through the process. It's how you maintain that initial momentum and dopamine-driven enthusiasm to keep them on the right path. If a patient's next in-office appointment is six months away, they will lose interest in their transformational responsibilities. Yes, it's their body and their health, but they have other things to do, and unless you give them regular reasons to stay engaged, that plan will fall to the bottom of their list of priorities.

Traction requires that you understand the type of interaction necessary to move your patients forward. Some appointments need to be with you to deploy or check in on your strategy, and many need to be with a health coach (in-person or on an app) to ensure that momentum and accountability is maintained. Design a traction plan for each phase of your transformational process and then decide on the type of tool or practitioner necessary for each encounter.

Note that, when you first start out in practice, you will likely be serving as coach and strategist, and that's okay. Still focus on understanding the functional needs of each encounter, so you know how to communicate your plan and eventually hand the responsibility of coaching and momentum to someone else on your team.

Investigation

According to data from 2019, Americans spent over $2 billion that year on psychics and related services. This is not a commentary on these choices, but rather on our inherent interest in acquiring unique insight about who we are...and our willingness to pay for it. When you deploy testing and objective measures as part of your process, you not only provide insight, but you also deliver context for their progress.

Examples of investigation could include functional testing, basic blood work, movement screens or questionnaires. Investigative tools should be considered in each phase of care, including Discovery. Show them how far they have come.

Remember, this is a framework—not a set of rules. How you go about the investigation piece is up to you, and there are many ways to accomplish the task. The key thing to remember is that people respond well to unique insights about themselves and their progress.

Others

The O in ACTION stands for Others that the patient sees about their health or that you refer them to for additional support. Being a part of referral networks helps you, and it helps the patient. Don't try to be everything to them. Effectively referring out, either as part of your process or as the need arises will solidify their confidence in your care and expertise. 'O' is a reminder to stay in your lane and actively communicate and coordinate with other providers.

Next Steps

The N in ACTION is for next steps—the regular communication you maintain with your patients and clear instructions on what they should expect. They should know the reason (function) for their upcoming appointments, not just the next one, but the next two at least. They should know why they're coming to see you for these appointments and what they can expect to gain from the experience. Imagine being a patient, sitting in a waiting room, not knowing why you're there, how long you'll be or how much it's going to cost . . . or when this seemingly endless pattern of appointments will end.

Your patient's time is valuable. If you bring them in for a visit and they don't know why they need to be there, their confidence in you wavers. Their excitement subsides. The same is true for any treatments you provide—why are you doing it, and what will they gain from each encounter? Your patients want to know. When it comes to next steps, there is no such thing as overcommunication regarding its function and context in your plan.

[Your Name Here] Framework

Once you have created your unique ACTION framework and methodology, name it. Make it your own. This is now your intellectual property and part of your brand. You can name it after yourself or make up a name that resonates with your clients.

Your framework is an asset that you can take with you wherever you go. Feel free to tweak it as your business grows. It's yours, and no one else's. Now put it to work.

THE LEGACY OF YOUR INTELLECTUAL PROPERTY

Building your practice, your processes and your skills is a lot of work. The value of what you create is a priceless reflection of your life's work. For some, the end of their journey means simply closing down their business. For others, there is a desire to sell or pass along their work. Creating a process and methodology provides you with an option to sell and package the intellectual property that encompasses your life's work and skill. For a business built on referrals and your charm as a practitioner, there are few assets that you can actually sell. Creating a methodology and process provides you with an asset and legacy related to your work that extends beyond you as a practitioner. It is one of the single most important things you can create for you and your future. It is your IP Legacy.

CHECK-IN

1. What outcome am I aiming to deliver?
2. What are the three to five pillars that I would need to address within a strategic care plan?
3. What eligibility criteria need to be in place for people to be successful as they move into the Active Phase of Care?
4. How frequently do I need to touch base with my patients for a strategic check-in? Coaching or momentum check-in? Any other form of interaction?
5. What will I name my methodology?

CHAPTER 12

MOVING FROM NEW IDEAS TO STRATEGIC ACTION

O n March 14, 2020, my phone blew up. Eight days prior, I had met with my mastermind group in person. The conversation was lively, and people were engaged. We were aware of the 'impending pandemic' but were still not sure how seriously our governments would be taking it. As we all departed, we hugged, shared cabs and carried on our way—blissfully unaware of what was to come.

In less than a week since our gathering, most of North America locked down. Practitioners were calling me in a panic.

Governments in both the US and Canada began initiating rules immediately in an effort to protect people in their countries from the rapid spread of the coronavirus, 'COVID-19', which had quickly disarmed slow-moving governments and healthcare systems. The virus created a complete separation between clinicians and their patients. We couldn't see people in our offices. We couldn't even have our own staff in our offices. In some areas, such as where I lived in Ontario, practitioners weren't even allowed to see patients virtually for fear that they would make recommendations that were off-script from the government narrative.

Practices that relied solely on one-to-one care lost their only source of income as governments limited access, even to virtual care. Patients who relied on one-to-one care were out of luck too—no more treatments. Unless the problem was an emergency, they would have to wait, and no one knew for how long.

Some clinicians had alternate avenues of health delivery—and alternate revenue streams. The restrictions caused by COVID-19 had a lesser effect on their businesses and their patients. They had actively cultivated a mailing list and amassed a following on social media. They had subscribers to their websites, blogs and other content. Instead of wringing their hands, they immediately reached out to their patients, quelling the panic, continuing current healthcare programmes and attracting many new patients to this alternate avenue of healthcare delivery.

Clinicians who had these communication channels in place held onto their patients and preserved at least a portion of their incomes. And they didn't panic . . . as much. They shifted gears a bit, moving more of their time to online health delivery, and while they slowed down, they didn't go broke. They also garnered deeper trust from their patients because they were there for them when many other people and services were not.

This isn't a criticism of practitioners who stuck with their belief that one-to-one treatment was never going away or who failed to adopt virtual care in a timely manner. The point is not that we don't need one-to-one care; it's that alone, it is a risk to our livelihood and a limitation on who we can reach.

If you can indulge me for a moment, I'll give you an example from a time before I learned this critical lesson. It was the first day of my four-day board exam. One section of the test was on botanical medicine, and *all* of the questions focussed on one particular plant—Lobelia (or possibly something else, but the particulars are irrelevant). I thought that it was odd, but when I sat down to study for the second day of the test, I figured there was no reason to review Lobelia again. That plant would likely never cross my path again, at least not on a test.

Imagine my surprise when, on day two, I opened my test booklet, and there it was: an entire section on Lobelia—again! Mentally kicking myself for not studying the plant when I had the chance, I finished the work, went home and studied for day three. Did I study Lobelia? Of course not. No test in the history of all tests would spend three days on the same damned plant when there were so many other, more dangerous botanicals I should know.

You can probably guess how that assumption played out for me on the third and final day of the test. Lobelia, one last time.

This makes for a great lesson now, but I was not laughing then. The practitioners who called me in a panic on March 14 weren't laughing either.

Don't let the pandemic be your Lobelia. We may not have to contend with a pandemic exactly like this ever again, but you *will* need to rely on diversified income in your lifetime. This should be your wake-up call.

GETTING STARTED WITH THE FOUR QUADRANTS OF CARE

In Chapter 10, I described the Quadrants of Care: Aspirational, Empowerment, Strategy and Growth. In addition to helping us categorize which stage a patient's in regarding their search for better health, the quadrants present practitioners with opportunities for diversified income. In order to earn this income, you must first diversify your offerings. For practitioners, that means expanding beyond the transactional approach to treating patients and beginning to acknowledge the unique needs of health consumers at each stage of their health journey. Let's take a look at each quadrant and how clinicians can approach and leverage them effectively.

Aspirational Quadrant

Through schooling and clinical training, practitioners are taught to be great one-to-one providers. But health promotion and lifestyle changes can be initiated even before a patient sets foot in your door. These changes can start in Quadrant 1: the Aspirational Quadrant.

Think of this first quadrant like this: Your potential patients are walking around in a marketplace going from stand to stand. Why are they going to stop at yours? What have you been doing to show that you have their best interests in mind? Your competition in the marketplace is not other practitioners; it's easier solutions. This is your opportunity to present your unique approach—why someone would want to invest their time and money in you versus taking an Advil or consuming more coffee.

The Aspirational Quadrant is where you solidify your foundation. Define your authority and speak directly to your ideal client. It's where you give away information and hint at the strategy you deliver for those who choose to work with you.

Empowerment (DIY) Quadrant

Next, after you've built that client foundation and made the mental shift towards transformational health delivery, you can and will naturally move your followers and fans into the Empowerment Quadrant.

In this quadrant, your raving fans will be looking to you to provide a deeper experience with respect to their health. They are likely not ready to jump into one-to-one care, but they are much more inclined to invest and try things on their own. In this phase, look for ways to capture content that you share over and over again, and put it in a format that you can deliver to more people than you've been doing in a one-to-one relationship. This is not a phase where you are addressing individualized needs. This quadrant is an opportunity to move the needle on a problem that is common to many of your patients. This quadrant is a place where you might offer a group programme on blood sugar regulation or eliminating gluten or an online course on managing eczema without medication. This is a place where you are organizing *information* into a strategic offering so that prospective health consumers can achieve an outcome on their own.

For many, this will be the first time they ever realized that they can control their health with their actions. This is not a stage we should begrudge as clinicians; it is a phase we should applaud. Teaching our patients to be a member of their own medical team is something we need to encourage. The best part about this phase is that the content or programme you create can be used again and again. This is called 'leverage', and it is how you will start to transition from a business model that is entirely predicated on selling your time for money.

At the lowest area of the triangle—the base, where the net is casting the widest—the level of content can be very general. At the top, the content is much more targeted. Regardless of where it falls on this triangle, your content benefits someone, and it benefits your business.

Regardless of where your content falls in the triangle, it's information you've provided more than once to more than a single patient in a one-to-one setting. Now that you've captured, crafted and shared it, you will never (hopefully) have to repeat the information again.

Strategy Quadrant

The best time to start leveraging your time was years ago, when you first started your practice. The second-best time is today.

Practitioners who fail to leverage their time suffer the most, burning out at alarming rates. These are the clinicians who scroll through text messages on their phones at night, catching up on a myriad of requests from patients. They get up at 4:00 a.m. to respond to emails because that's the only 'free' time they'll have all day to do that task. The rest of the day, they're with patients or charting their endless interactions.

When these practitioners aren't treating patients, they're trying to sell them a next visit. They're worried about patient retention, and they should be. Without a transformational plan in place that engages the patient in their own whole-body, long-term wellness, every visit to your office is like another deal you have to close.

Establishing your transformational process in the Strategic Quadrant is where most practitioners should focus first. This is your most expensive and exclusive offering, and it remains the anchor in the ecosystem of care offerings.

For case studies around the deployment of programming and offerings in each of these quadrants, visit impactmedicinebook.com/resources.

Growth Quadrant

Practitioners help more people not by lowering our fees (or raising them indiscriminately), but by innovating our offering. By combining what is most beneficial to the patient and what makes practitioners utilize their time most efficiently, impactful ways of transforming the current model of care and patient outcomes are happening every day.

Case Study:
Dr. Michelle Peris, ND

Dr. Michelle Peris, a Canadian Naturopathic Doctor and clinician entrepreneur, executed this concept brilliantly. She created an offering called the Wild Collective, a women's group care programme based on her teachings on mindset, self-actualization and women's health curriculum. Michelle gathered women patients in her office for these initial meetings, and the women soon began bringing their friends. The group grew, and Michelle offered them DIY content they could use outside of the in-office meetings. These women were engaged, discussing what they learned in the meetings and outside the group as well. Eventually, Michelle brought in associates to help her run the group. She created more intellectual property for these associates to share, and they brought more women into the collective. Referrals poured in, more sessions were organized, and that one group of women expanded beyond Michelle's office. The Wild Collective spread like wildfire, and dozens of clinics across North America began to share the Wild Collective with their patient communities as well. Each one uses Dr. Peris's practices and content, and she gets paid for all of it. Michelle doesn't need to maintain her private practice, and she doesn't need to take board exams in every jurisdiction where her Wild Collective is practiced. She simply licensed the brand and the intellectual property and made it available to other practitioners. Everyone wins. Everyone continues to grow. So can you.

CHECK-IN

1. Where do I currently have 'low hanging fruit' in my practice? (For example, do you have a particular type of patient that would benefit from a group or online programme?)

2. What do I wish all of my one-to-one patients knew or had achieved with respect to their health *before* they set foot in my door?

3. Do I have an experience or offering that I can send my patients towards when they are 'done' with one-to-one care? If not, what do I think might be exciting or keep them engaged?

CHAPTER 13

USER EXPERIENCE (UX)

One day, working in my downtown office, I could feel the slow insidious onset of a headache. Opting for self-care over Advil, I decided to get a massage. In Toronto, massage clinics are like coffee shops—they're everywhere. Short on time, I booked one close to my office.

Approaching the reception desk, I noticed how tired the office was looking—the horrible paint colour and peeling stickers on the walls. If I had had more time, I probably would have turned on my heel, but my headache was getting worse, and I just wanted to get rid of the pain and go back to work. I was also trying not to judge a book by its cover.

I was invited into a treatment room, which was even worse than the waiting room. Dust and cobwebs clung to the corners, and the light was broken and leaning precariously to one side. There wasn't a single attractive piece of décor in the whole drab, dreary—and actually quite dirty—place. Mind you, this wasn't a TV repair shop. It was a chiropractic clinic. A place that you would expect to find radiate peace and tranquillity. I wasn't feeling any of that. I should have left, but I stayed out of curiosity—and pain. I looked closely at the massage table and could see the sheets were clean and pressed. Someone had at least taken care of that detail.

The massage was okay, but nothing to write home about. The massage therapist all but ignored my attempts to start a conversation. I was keen on making connections with people and networking, so I told the therapist a little bit about my occupation. My office, after all, was a block away.

Crickets.

I never went back.

After the experience, I couldn't help but think how badly I wanted to makeover that whole place—the whole *experience*. I thought about my conversation—or lack thereof—with the massage therapist. I had mentioned my nearby practice and the fact that I was always on the lookout for referral partners. Basically, I was gauging the person's interest in sending me clients and vice versa (though honestly, would I really send my patients to that place?). Still, if someone walked into my office with that kind of offer, I'd jump on it. We'd be having lunch or grabbing a coffee, discussing the possibilities.

My disappointment with the situation all boiled down to user experience, or 'UX' for short. Health consumers want a good user experience, and you owe it to them to deliver one. Take pride in your office, your staff and yourself. Show your patients that you care enough to go the extra mile and give them a pleasant, consistent experience with every interaction. This attention to detail builds trust...and referrals.

UX FOR THE PATIENT

Assess your patients' current user experience. Walk through the entire process at your practice, from the parking lot through the front door, to reception, the waiting and treatment rooms, virtual or otherwise. What's it like to be your patient? How does it *feel*?

Then, think about what you can do to make it better. In addition to cosmetic changes, consider how long people wait in your office, the people with whom they interact, the process of completing paperwork and so forth. Is it a pleasant experience, or is it cumbersome and confusing?

Rewrite the experience, step by step, from start to finish. Then, make it happen. When my team and I did this exercise at our clinic, our strategy focussed on the patient's emotions. How did they feel interacting with our practice?

The changes we made weren't complicated or expensive. One of the first things we did was initiate two touchpoints with new patients who had scheduled an appointment with us, by email and by phone. We would let them know that we'd be sending along emails that would introduce them to our practice and help them prepare for their appointment. We knew that people don't always read every email, and we wanted to make sure they read ours and that they understood that we were anticipating their visit—looking forward to it, in fact.

We didn't want new patients walking into the office feeling lost and alone. In the email, we included a link to a short video showing them how to complete the intake forms and explaining why the information we gathered was necessary, and how it would make our time together more effective and efficient. We also included a summary of what would happen during the visit, for example, whether a physical exam was included or necessary.

Pre-appointment emails are a great, non-confrontational way to explain the rules and regulations of your office too. For example, do you allow children or pets in the waiting room? Are masks required? Is hand sanitiser available, and do you recommend they use it? Consider all the questions a patient has and answer them ahead of the appointment. People like to feel confident in new spaces.

After the first appointment, I send additional emails to help explain what's next for the patient—processes, treatments and other activities coming up in future visits. I'm conscious of the Quadrants of Care, and I nurture the patients through each one, as they're ready. My objective is not to control the patient but to slowly hand control to them—to empower them to take an active, managerial role in their own health. This shift changes their attitude towards health and towards the practitioner. They see you as a partner in their healthcare instead of someone who takes their money and tells them what to do.

THE INFORMATION TO SHARE

The information you share with your patients will never be static. Regardless of the avenue in which you choose to send information

—text, emails, videos, phone calls—it will always be evolving.

Brainstorm the questions patients ask you and look for commonalities. Consider which of these questions can be answered with a page on your website or by updating those initial videos you send, introducing new patients to the practice. Look for procedures that are new, or at least new to patients, that you can explain in a video or by other means. Include a walk-through of your offices and the exam rooms, so they feel like they're entering a place they're familiar with, and are more at ease. Before you do this, make sure you've applied those cosmetic changes we talked about—no ugly walls and peeling stickers.

Your first videos won't be perfect, but that's okay. Don't let that deter you. Analysis paralysis can prevent you from moving forward, but only if you let it. You can revise the videos over time and make new ones—the important thing is to do it. Do it *soon*.

Have fun with these videos. Let your personality show through. Give them fun titles. They should be professional, sure, but they shouldn't be stuffy or sterile. These are people coming to your office, not robots. They want to know that you're a person too. The goal is to make them feel comfortable. *Empowered*. Take away the fear of the unknown so that when they sit down in your observation room, they are totally at ease and able to focus on their health.

The user experience can break trust, such as my experience at the massage clinic, or it can help build it. Put yourself into it. Make it your own. This can be the first step in developing a brand that permeates everything you do as you create a thriving business and an engaging practice that you and your patients love.

For a checklist related to perfecting your user experience, visit impactmedicinebook.com/resources.

CHECK-IN

1. Move through the experience your patients experience. What communication, visuals and touchpoints would augment their interaction and make them feel more confident before their visit?

2. What do you wish patients knew before their first visit? Is this something you can create content for?

PART THREE:
P OF PATIENTS—KEY TAKEAWAYS

The way we build health is different than the way we manage disease. The new, transformational model can become the medicine itself. You have the potential to deliver healthcare to more people, exert a greater influence over them, empower them to engage more passionately in their own health plan and build your business exponentially. You will not get there solely with one-to-one care. There's a better way, and it's within your reach. You can do this.

For more IMPACT Medicine resources, visit
impactmedicinebook.com/resources.

PART FOUR

ATTRACTION

'Courage starts with showing up and
letting ourselves be seen'.

—Brené Brown

did not grow up wanting to be a Naturopathic Doctor. I was set on becoming a litigator or a fighter pilot. When I was fired from a summer job for refusing to scrub a public washroom that had not been attended to for nearly twenty years, I decided that I would start my own business. In my little tin boat, I offered cottage cleaning services to vacationers at their island properties. The business took off, and I soon found myself spending summers on the dock while driving my friends to clean the cabins of my island-dwelling clients. I would never have a 'real job' again.

Around the same time, I was experiencing debilitating menstrual cramps. Pummeled with birth control pills, Depo Provera, three surgeries and countless specialists, I was running out of steam. When a new doctor finally recommended that I try a medication called Lupron to induce menopause in my sixteen-year-old body, I declared that enough was enough. I would find a better solution myself because *this* solution felt like over-reach. Surely, the human body was capable of more without the use of such suppressive therapies. I was right.

My parents were very open-minded when it came to medicine. When someone, a friend of the family, suggested taking me to a Naturopathic Doctor, there were no objections. 'Sure, I'll try anything', my mother said.

This new doctor explained how Naturopathic Medicine works—but I wasn't really listening. I was still stuck and struck by the intelligence of the question he asked when I first walked into the room:

'How has your body always and historically responded to stress'? It was the smartest question anybody had ever asked me about my health.

This new line of questioning opened the door to new options for healing my body. I changed my diet, complied with remedies, came off all medications and learned how to trust my body. I was telling everyone who would listen about Naturopathic Medicine... and my new choice of careers. I was going to study Naturopathic Medicine, and I was going to combine it with my natural state of 'unemployability'. I was going to become a clinician entrepreneur.

Most practitioners don't like to market themselves. It feels inauthentic, salesy or cheap. Our schooling doesn't promote the idea of marketing either. Instead, it emphasizes education and credentials as a prudent path towards credibility. But credibility alone won't lead patients into your practice. Renting an office and putting your name on the door isn't good enough. Nobody knows who you are, where you are, or what you do. No one knows that you're the most qualified person to treat them and put them on the path towards health optimization. *You have to get in front of people and let them know.* Naturopathic Medicine changed my life, and I don't begrudge a single piece of marketing that moved me closer to finding my first practitioner. Marketing is an act of service that moves the right people towards an option that could change their life. Why would you hesitate in denying people that opportunity?

I got lucky when my parents came across the suggestion to see a new type of doctor, in my case, one who knew the right question to ask. Most people don't simply stumble upon the right clinician. As a practitioner, you know you have a powerful solution to people's problems—why are you not out there shouting it from the rooftops? You spent hundreds of thousands of dollars and sacrificed countless years of your life to become the provider you are today. Don't let it go to waste. Don't assume that the sacrifice alone is what will drive clients to your door, because it won't.

Healthcare is extremely specialized. Once you've identified your Arena of Authority (niche), you need a system of attraction to draw people to your practice. The only way to move the needle is by seeking and identifying your ideal clientele and reaching out to them through a trust and marketing system. Your biggest competition is your own silence. A rigorous system of attraction is how you defeat that competition and grow what will become your greatest asset—the ability to reach and influence the people you want to help.

Within the word 'attraction' is another word: 'traction'. You need traction to create and maintain a connection with the patients you want to help. The five Ts of Traction bring clarity to marketing your business, taking you another step closer to harnessing your inner clinician entrepreneur.

1. **Target:** You need a target audience, your niche market. Casting a wide net may seem like the best way to attract the most people, but you can't help everybody and even if you could (which you can't), you wouldn't be able to help all of them as well as they deserve.

2. **Transformation:** Don't talk about one-and-done fixes—communicate the complete health transformation that you deliver for patients.

3. **Trust:** Reinforce trust at every touchpoint with your patients. Be intentional about your clarity in messaging, the quality of your brand and your focus on optimizing the patient experience. Clarity around your Arena of Authority is one of the fastest unspoken ways of solidifying trust.

4. **Traffic:** Develop a strategy and a system for consistently driving people to your business.

5. **Tools (for conversion):** Enlist tools that convert people within each of the Four Quadrants of Care to the next quadrant.

We'll get into each of these traction tools deeper in this Part.

Your ideal client doesn't know about you or your Arena of Authority. It's your job to find them, educate them and show them why you are the person they need to come to for the optimized health they are seeking. You can't just wait for them to stumble upon you. You need to attract new clients by building your audience and, in turn, your business, as you make the transition from practitioner to clinician entrepreneur.

CHAPTER 14

MESSAGING

I once worked with a Functional Medicine practitioner who was great at providing information, terrible at messaging. Sam (not his real name) was passionate about sharing his knowledge with his online followers. He posted daily videos (which in theory, is a great strategy—practitioners tend to avoid video more than anything else, and they also struggle with that kind of marketing consistency, so kudos to Sam), but his efforts didn't generate nearly the results one would expect. Sam's videos were plentiful but poorly produced. The background was unattractive, the sound quality was inconsistent, and his lighting and camera work were unintentionally deployed. Viewers were treated to a dimly lit close-up of Sam's nose and muffled voice, which distracted them from his valuable information.

In addition to visual issues with Sam's videos, the words he used and treatments he described were beyond a typical patient's vocabulary or understanding. He spoke with such a high level of detail and medical knowledge that only a fellow practitioner would be able to understand what he was saying. He secretly admitted to being more consumed with what his colleagues were thinking than selecting language that would resonate with his desired audience.

Sam had the right idea. He was trying to share his knowledge with the hope that it would help viewers. People (mostly women) watched his videos, hoping for answers, but they were turned off by the quality. The funny thing was that Sam was really smart, and he knew his subject matter inside and out. He had great advice for anyone who dared click on a video with a thumbnail of a close-up nose, sit through a whole viewing and decipher his message. Needless to say, Sam had a low number of followers and even worse conversions. Sam's smart messaging and the effort he put into his videos were wasted.

My team and I worked with Sam to overhaul his messaging strategy. We helped him create aesthetically pleasing videos with an attractive background, good lighting and better camera placement. We helped him alter the message, using a layperson's vocabulary that made prospective patients feel smart instead of confused. We also enlisted a strategy called the JK 5 that was created by marketing guru Jenna Kutcher, which I'll explain in more detail in the next chapter.[7]

The result of this messaging makeover was nothing short of explosive. Sam's new videos were pleasing to look at and listen to.

---

7   Jenna Kutcher, 'The Secret Behind My Most Liked Instagram Posts EVER', Jenna Kutcher Blog, https://jennakutcherblog.com/most-liked/.

By showing people that he cared enough about them to present an image that was easy to watch, focus on what they needed and talk about it in language they understood, his userbase skyrocketed. He gained momentum and attracted more followers, and in time, his business thrived. His videos were doing their job; they were adding clarity and credibility to his credentials, providing results for his audience and instilling trust in those looking to invest more deeply in their health.

THE ANATOMY OF YOUR MESSAGE

Your message is your conviction around your process and the system of medicine that you practice. That conviction needs to emerge in everything you do. It needs to show itself in the way you nurture your email list, how you show up on social media and how your website is designed. Consistency of messaging supports the strength of your personal or clinic brand and does its number-one job of establishing trust.

Establishing trust can happen in many ways. In the realm of marketing, it starts with consistent Foundational Messaging. Foundational Messaging consists of three core ingredients: your Authority Statement, your World View and indoctrination.

Let's start with your Authority Statement. Instilling trust between you and those for whom you have the potential to help isn't about being relatable to everybody. It's about being relatable only to those people you are targeting. To design your message, ask yourself, *What is the pain point of my target audience, and what is the solution they are looking for?*

In the book *Building a StoryBrand*, author Donald Miller introduces a concept that allows you to simplify your message for the people you're trying to reach.[8] Once you gain clarity on your offer and audience, simplifying your message into an 'Authority Statement', such as the one that follows, will add clarity and, by extension, credibility to what you do.

I take _____ (your ideal client avatar) from _____ (problem) to _____ (solution) using _____ (your specialized method).

The entire idea behind this message is not to lay out your credentials or to prove how smart you are. This message isn't about you at all; it's about cultivating curiosity through a sense of confidence. Once you complete that statement, you should have clarity on who you serve and in what way. Refinement of your Authority Statement and the beliefs and values that inform your mission are something I call your 'World View'.

Your World View is the background that informs your Authority Statement. Think about the values, experiences and beliefs that drove you towards your career and the population you have chosen to serve.

What is *your* World View?

What is the core underlying belief that informs your work?

---

8 Donald Miller, Building a StoryBrand: Clarify Your Message So Customers Will Listen (New York: HarperCollins Leadership, 2017).

What is your 'why'?

For me, I believe that when people have their health, they can change the world. That is the 'why' behind the work that I do. It's why I am in the arena of healthcare that I am in and why I work so hard to put our systems of medicine into the hands of millions of people. Frankly, I won't engage with a business that doesn't support that World View. And, my worldview attracts people who share a similar set of values.

Your prospective patients want to have a deeper understanding of your 'why'. Crafting an Authority Statement with your World View in mind distinguishes your messaging and solidifies your place with an audience that shares your values. When your ideal audience sees your online videos or social media posts, they should be able to feel what you feel and believe in what you're saying.

If you're struggling to get started, write down ten belief statements. Go way back to the beginning. Think about the day you decided it was worth your time and money to obtain the education you did. What drove you to stay in school even when you thought about quitting? Use those core beliefs to inform the emotion behind your Authority Statement.

Remember, there are three core elements to your Foundational Messaging: your beliefs and World View, your Authority Statement and indoctrination.

If you have attracted people who believe what you believe (World View) and need what you are offering (Authority Statement), it is time to teach them more about your Arena of Authority and expertise. I call this teaching 'indoctrination'. This is where your audience transitions to becoming your biggest fans. This is not about making you look smart; this is about making your audience feel smarter for following along. Clarifying your Foundational Messaging will enable you to have greater focus as you build the more sophisticated elements of your marketing system and attract more and more of your ideal clients towards your offerings.

YOU ARE ALWAYS MARKETING

Practitioners are comfortable delivering care. Ideally, we solve health problems—come up with answers to our patients' questions and send them on their way to happier, healthier lives.

At least that's what we say we want to do . . . The reality for many is that our fear or hesitation of marketing ourselves and an outcome leaves us stuffing as much value as possible into our first few interactions of an inconsistent flow of patients. While this may not be true for you, it happens with sufficient frequency that it poses a significant threat to the rise of unqualified 'influencers' as prominent voices in health. A business is predicated on a few critical components. First and foremost, you need a product or service of value, in this case your care/credentials. Secondly, a business requires a marketing system, operations strategy and revenue capacity. There are no exceptions. You might not want to market, but it is the noble act of putting your service into the hands of those who need it.

Early on in my career, I was guilty of the practice of marketing-avoidance-at-all-costs. I wanted so badly to make sure my patients knew that they had complete power over whether or not they were going to come back to see me again, and I didn't want their decision to feel influenced in any way. I would mount a huge amount of effort to secure a talk or exposure opportunity to attract new patients, but I would fail to position our work together as a transformational experience. I sold the required effort, investment and outcome short. The result was new patients that wouldn't stick around past three or four visits. I didn't know what to do because my patient–practitioner relationship was built on trust, and I didn't want patients to think I was trying to 'sell them'. I was dragging my own limiting ideas and baggage about sales into our relationship, and it was negatively affecting their outcomes. When done with compassion and honesty, *selling* actually builds more trust. I was so worried that my patients would feel 'sold to' that what they got was nowhere... Even the ones who really wanted what I was offering.

What I failed to consider was that these patients came to me for a reason. That they wanted the *best* care I could provide. The best did not mean the fastest or the most densely packed with information. If they heard me speak and followed up, they were obviously intrigued enough to make an appointment and show up. They wanted further reassurance that I could deliver on the promise of my talk or presentation. In this case, integrity was about delivering on the promise of putting a viable and important option in their hands. This would require that I had to get past my hang-up and hesitation around sales. Sharing the value of my training and its potential to impact people's health was my life's calling. If I wasn't willing to talk about it and move people in the direction of this option, I would be denying potential patients an amazing opportunity for better health. I wasn't selling a product that lacked integrity.

I needed to place more confidence in the health consumer's capacity to decide on the best option forward for themselves. Hedging and avoiding sales and marketing was an outward admission that I didn't believe that consumers had the capacity to make their own informed choices. My patients' perceptions of the value and process was something I needed to be aware of, but it was not necessarily something I had a responsibility to alter.

As a new practitioner, when patients came in to see me, I went above and beyond to make them feel like they weren't being 'sold' on anything. But I went too far. And that wasn't my job. In fact, my job was the opposite. I tried so hard to prevent myself from sounding like I was selling them that I actually drove them away. They wanted me to prove to them that I was going to solve their problems—to have the answers they were seeking to the lingering problems they were facing. I could do that, and more, but I held myself back.

There's a built-in belief that our competition is other healthcare providers, but that isn't the case. Our real competition is the faster, simpler and more expedited way our patients can solve their problems. If someone is dealing with chronic migraines or menstrual cramps and they come to our office, we shouldn't be nervous to discuss our capacity for assistance. If we have the ability to address their condition but are too afraid to tell them what it will take, we risk losing them to the competition, Advil. You owe it to those you seek to serve to get clear on your messaging regarding how you can help. If you cannot properly relay your message to your patients, then they will lack the opportunity to make an informed decision about their health.

As clinician entrepreneurs, our messaging and the consistency with which we share it are critical. Whether we are aware of it or not, some message is being taken in by our patients. We can either have that message be one that brings us closer to working together, or farther away.

WHEN SELLING IS SLEAZY

Most people can detect when they're being *sold*. It's why most practitioners don't want to try to sell to health consumers—they feel like they're being placed into that category of 'sleazy salesperson' or unethically pushing people towards an option that is not their choice.

Your patients are always being sold, though. If it isn't you doing the selling, somebody else will be, and that's who'll get to your patient and their health. That somebody else could be a pharmaceutical company with an easy answer, an Instagram influencer with an uninformed approach or a colleague who has worked through their confidence with marketing and sales. If you have a solution that you believe will change people's lives, you *get* to address the limitations in mindset that are holding you back from the care and impact you provide.

Selling is unethical and especially uncomfortable when you push people to spend their money on things they don't need. If you do sales the right way, you are helping them strive towards a healthcare objective and option that benefits them. You are helping them come to their own conclusion to make the right decision on their own. This is the ultimate goal: to empower people to make powerful choices about their health and well-being.

WITH MORE TRUST, THERE IS LESS SELLING

The goal of your messaging is to instil trust and relatability. But that messaging does not need to come just from you. Including positive reviews, testimonials (in jurisdictions where this is allowed) and other forms of social proof is an effective way of reinforcing your credibility. Social proof can include the opinions of others in the form of testimonials or an acknowledgement of your history of credibility in the marketplace. Share the logos from media outlets, stages or podcasts where you have appeared as another creative way to support this narrative.

Establishing trust and credibility comes down to knowing your ideal audience and the outcome they are looking to achieve. This combination is your Arena of Authority. Maintaining trust and expertise in this arena requires clear consistent messaging and an unwavering commitment towards moving the right people into your system of care. When you've got this in order, you are ready to move on to the next stage of your marketing strategy: developing *you* as the brand.

CHECK-IN

1. How would I define my Arena of Authority (niche + ideal client)?
2. What are the core beliefs that inform why I do the work I do in this world?
3. Brainstorm five quick ways you could elevate your authority and trust immediately on your website, social media and other public profiles.

4. Define your Authority Statement:

I take _____

from _____ *to* _____

using _____.

5. What limiting beliefs related to sales and marketing are holding me back from reaching the people I know I can impact?

CHAPTER 15

YOU AS THE BRAND

V anessa runs a successful public relations firm with a long client roster. I met with her to talk about my personal brand and how I could gain more exposure.

'Tell me about your brand', she said, 'in just three words'. I paused for a moment, and as well as I thought I knew what I was about, I couldn't answer her question. Not in three words. Not even in a hundred, apparently.

'Well, I have *this* business, and I have *that* business', I said, 'and then I have my own personal brand that sort of works within them'. I knew my businesses and how they worked together, but I wasn't answering Vanessa's question. She knew it too.

At the end of our conversation, she shared, 'This has been great, but I still don't know what your brand is about. I don't understand its *essence*'. I was confused and a little defensive, but then she explained, 'What I want you to do is to describe your brand in three words. I want to know what it feels like'. That gave me clarity around the task and motivated me to give it another shot.

After our meeting, I thought about how I could condense my brand into three words, but the task seemed impossible. I had too many different businesses—too many different things going on. How could I pull them together and be concise enough to describe it in just three words?

I had to take a step back and really think about what Vanessa had said. She was asking me about *my* brand. About my *personal* brand. That realization made me think about the question in a different light. This one compelling conversation changed the trajectory of how I thought about who I was professionally and the focus required to create concise clarity.

My brand wasn't the clinic's brand or the business's brand. My brand was me. Once I realized this, everything became clearer. I no longer sounded like such a hot, confused mess. I actually knew what I was talking about. And the confidence I now brought into my conversations with people was showing. With my clarity came the trust that people had in my message. My businesses and the things I did in the world were no longer confusing—everything was, well, on-brand.

Branding and messaging aren't the same thing. Your message tells the story of what you do. It explains the pain of your ideal client, how you treat them and the outcome.

Your brand is what allows people to immediately distinguish you and your company from others. It's how you show up in the world: how you dress and speak, your values, what you believe and what matters to you. The two—messaging and brand—are related, but they're separate too. In essence, your brand informs your messaging, and your messaging echoes your brand.

RULE OF THREE

The Rule of Three, a concept I used in the process of defining my own brand, asks the clinician entrepreneur to select three fonts, three colours and three words to define their personal and/or clinic brand. These elements, nine in total, are your unique identifiers and a starting point to projecting a consistent brand 'tone'. Consistency strengthens your brand and ensures you can replicate your tones, colours and fonts with intention. Your brand guide should contain a detailed reference to all of your brand constituents and the information required for anyone to replicate the look and feel of your brand. The Rule of Three provides a handy starting point for the elements you need to consider for your brand guide. It represents you to the outside world and communicates who you are and what you are about.

Any images you create, from your logo to your website design to your video backgrounds, should include your brand elements. Your brand guide may change over time, but not without careful consideration. Store it, along with images such as your logo, fonts and supporting graphics, in a place where the people who work with you on all of your messaging can access it readily. Make sure they understand its importance and its use.

Your brand guide can also include your company's domain name or URL, any redirects that you have set up that drive people to your site from specific marketing efforts, and all social media handles assigned to your company. This includes professional sites like LinkedIn, social networking sites like Instagram and video channels like YouTube. Use handles that are easy to spell, easy to pronounce and easy to find. Ideally, keep them the same across all channels.

You can take this even further by creating a brand guide for yourself as an individual, separate from your business or clinic where you serve as an associate. Your personal brand guide should include the name of your personal website—ideally, your own name—and your personal social and professional networking site handles.

The greatest entrepreneurs have personal brands in addition to the brand(s) of their companies. Elon Musk has his own brand, separate from Tesla and SpaceX. Richard Branson has his own brand separate from Virgin. They know the power of leveraging themselves as a brand outside of their companies. The companies and the personal brands have a reciprocal relationship. But let's be honest, we are not Elon Musk or Richard Branson . . . yet. We do not currently have thousands of global employees or teams of brand and social media managers. It will be difficult for you to maintain and grow your personal and clinic brands. If you are at a stage where you can choose, lean into the development of your own brand first. People buy from people. You will gain more traction and opportunity from building you and your public persona as a priority first.

Over time, adhering to a brand guide trains people to distinguish your company from others at a glance. Defining simple fonts and colours are a great place to start. Over time, your ongoing growth and credibility will require that you invest in the cohesion and professionalism of your brand. Professional photos and branding are an important consideration as you place yourself at the front and centre of your work and message.

Above all else, creating a clean, professional and consistent brand is a requirement in today's online world. It's the difference between a brown, white and blue truck stopping in front of your home to drop off a delivery. You know immediately, without reading the name on the side of the truck whether you're getting a package from UPS, FedEx or Amazon.

All of this consistency demonstrates professionalism and communicates trust. It establishes a set of principles that clearly define your business and puts people at ease, knowing exactly what they will be getting with each interaction. Most importantly, for you, it empowers you to answer with 100 per cent clarity and confidence those compelling questions: *Who are you, and what do you do? Can you communicate the essence of who you are as a brand in three words?*

Mine are 'colourful', 'qualified' and 'impactful'.

BE IN CONTROL

Social media is a complicated place. It can be a force for good or a tool for torment. Regardless of where you stand (on any given day), the truth remains that social media is an important and powerful tool for showcasing your brand and message.

Whether it's the fear of being on camera, the imposter syndrome that sometimes comes with sharing knowledge or simply not having the time to put together a plan, there is almost always an excuse for why brands are not built, personal or otherwise in the online space.

Whether you want a personal brand or not, you have one. If you don't control your brand, someone else will. Competing practices will set themselves apart by creating a persona for you. They may not call you out by name, but the implication is clear in their brand and messaging. Other businesses might market their values relative to what they assume yours to be, and with no brand and no messaging, you won't have a defensive leg to stand on. When you don't engage, you have no control over your own narrative.

Your commitment to brand strengthens not only the trust and credibility of yourself and your business but of your industry. A rising tide lifts all ships, right? The more awareness you bring to your practice, the more awareness you bring to IMPACT Medicine and its benefits to the people we are all trying to help. That makes you more than a clinician entrepreneur. It can be the springboard towards thought leadership and provide radical distribution of your life-changing ideas.

While you can reach more people through a tool like social media, to really grow your business, you need to deploy a strategy to drive consistent traffic through your door.

CHECK-IN

1. How would I define my brand in three words or less? (Mine are 'colourful', 'qualified' and 'impactful'.)
2. What are the three fonts and colours that define my visual consistency?
3. Be honest: is my personal brand being represented with the level of professionalism that I want in the online space?

CHAPTER 16

TRAFFIC, CONVERSION AND COPY

My husband, a trained medical doctor who has also evolved beyond clinical practice, has retained a unique talent. He has an uncanny ability to rapidly develop deep and unyielding rapport with others. I can watch from across the room as he holds space to receive people's deepest secrets and confessions... whether he wants them or not. I'm convinced that this skill is less about being a great conversationalist and more about being a great listener. More importantly, Greg's listening skills are all the more powerful because so many of us are such *poor* listeners. Witnessing others and their experiences is becoming a lost art in our world of expedited communication, and those who have retained and cultivated this skill are inherent leaders and healers.

A common criticism of Naturopathic Medicine is that its success is predicated on the effective listening and attention provided by the practitioners. This sentiment does not explain the entirety of its success, but listening to patients should not be discounted as a contributing factor in one's healing. In fact, I would argue that traditional medicine is ill-equipped to handle the burden of chronic illness because of its systemic incapacity to listen to patients. Pills and pharmaceuticals become simple interventions when the system at-large lacks the time capacity to inspire, support and manage the lifestyle interventions that could save hundreds of thousands of lives per year. And yet, my goal isn't to start a war of the specialities. Instead, it's to find the most efficient methods for delivering health to health consumers and to share those systems in the hope of affecting better clinical outcomes.

While listening accelerates many facets of healing, one of the most critical is in its expedited capacity to cultivate trust. In an era where people can google their way towards a medical degree, establishing trust with our patients is critical to both our marketing and our delivery of care. Patient surveys over the last two decades show an increase in the overall satisfaction of care but a sharp decrease in trust with physicians across all specialities. While the paternalistic approach of the 1970s has been replaced with concerns about conflict of interest, eroding sentiments of trust risk undermining the delivery of effective transformation.[9]

Alarming? It sure is. But much of the medical community still operates with an assumption that trust is a byproduct of credentials,

---

9   Steven D. Pearson and Lisa H. Raeke, 'Patients' Trust in Physicians: Many Theories, Few Measures, and Little Data', Journal of General Internal Medicine 15 (July 2000): 5019–513, https://doi.org/10.1046/j.1525-1497.2000.11002.x.

and that credentialed advice should not be questioned. Yet, as you likely know, this idea isn't necessarily met by patients. Instead, 66 per cent of people doubt their providers. Nearly seven of every ten people you see in your practice do not necessarily trust what you say. This is our opportunity to stand out.

Even if they don't, people want to trust you. They know their life would be easier if they could. Or, even better, if you did something to expedite that process. You don't have to be the most popular person at the dinner party or have the mad skills to build the kind of rapport that has strangers telling you their deepest darkest secrets. You have the distinct advantage by being a practitioner—someone that people really want to trust. All you have to do is live up to, or exceed, their expectations.

THE IMPORTANCE OF TRUST

Health is deeply personal. Yet, health consumers are finding fewer personal ways to meet their health goals. The days of 'trust me, I'm a doctor—you can tell me anything' are being replaced by online sites packed with medical information and a slew of pharmaceuticals ads that promise to cure everything from hangnails to heart failure. Why would a patient come into your office and spill their guts to you about their most personal matters when they could simply order a treatment online or drop by their local pharmacy for a pill? In addition to this myriad of options, patients have come to think of practitioners as people they visit when they have a problem. They've bought into the pathogenic model of care. The modern practitioner trying to build a transformational model is up against a system that has been in place for so long that introducing this preventable model, one that better serves the patient, is sometimes met with scepticism. This is one more reason why messaging and branding are so important. The confidence and credibility you portray with consistency goes a long way towards establishing trust with patients and makes it much easier for them to accept this new model of care.

Part of this is your professionalism, but it's also your willingness to show people that you're a person too, with pains, challenges and vulnerabilities just like theirs. This makes you instantly relatable—someone like them, who can do things like they do. Achieving this does not mean you have to be an open book. You don't need to lay your entire life out on social media for all to see. There's a limit to what should be shared, and I liken that to wound care. You don't need to show everyone the open wound, but you can show them the scar tissue. Scar tissue shows that the wound was there, and the lesson was learned. Showing the open wound, on the other hand, will probably just drive people away.

Trust takes a long time to build. Your brand and messaging allow you to slowly build this trust over time without having to speak with every potential patient face-to-face. They are tools for efficiency.

While it takes a long time to build trust, it can be wiped away in a second. There is no turning back from a lack of trust. Once the door is closed, patients won't open up to you in the way they should. They won't be vulnerable themselves, telling you about past medical conditions or unhealthy habits. Trust is both a tool for marketing and care. Without it, neither one is possible.

THE TRAFFIC TRIFECTA

Whether or not you own your practice, you are responsible for driving your own traffic, the patients you bring into the business. One more time, for the people in the back: it is not the responsibility of anyone else to build a traffic strategy for your business. Anything promised by a clinic is a bonus. Driving traffic used to mean bringing people to your front door. It was predicated on a fancy A-frame sign, a Yellow Pages ad or even a listing in an online platform like Yelp. Nowadays, driving traffic means directing people towards your website, mailing list and eventually your booking link.

At its most simple level, I divide traffic into three distinct opportunities called the 'Traffic Trifecta': paid traffic, social traffic and relationship traffic. Each element of the trifecta drives traffic to you, your business and your brand.

Paid Traffic

Paid traffic is an advanced move. It is not the first line option that most practitioners or businesses should reach for, but it bears mentioning. Paid traffic comes from Google Ads and listings, social media ads and retargeting. Paid traffic can be generated by two different strategies.

Intention-based paid traffic is the result you achieve when you go looking for things on search engines like Google. It is valuable because it shows your offering to people who are poised and ready to take the next step.

Demographic-driven paid traffic is the type of traffic you generate when you pay for ads on a platform such as Instagram. In this case, you are aiming to intersect with your ideal client, and you are hoping that they take the marketing bait. This type of traffic generation takes longer and requires more nurturing before the 'cold traffic' generally makes the decision to purchase.

Paid traffic should be considered once your offer, brand and marketing infrastructure are in place and proven. Spending money on traffic before you have a proven offer is not the best use of your precious capital.

At any given moment, you can invest your money or your time in your business. If you are not paying for traffic, there are two other important considerations.

Social Traffic

Ah, social media. The amazing marketing tool we love to hate. Here's the unfortunate truth. As a small business owner, you wear two hats: (1) practitioner/professional and (2) content creator. Social media remains one of the most effective and proven tools to drive new patients towards our practices.

If reaching more people with your message and mission is what you are looking to do, social media will be a critical tool to help you reach your goal. Remember, in one-to-one practice, you sell your strategy. The dissemination and distribution of information lives in the realm of social media. As the quality of information you share continues to grow, so too does your authority and trust with you audience. As a primary tool in the Aspirational Quadrant, sharing social content has three primary goals—build trust, drive authority and move people onto your mailing list and deeper into your practice.

Relationship Traffic

The third component of the Traffic Trifecta is relationship traffic, a powerful yet underutilized traffic driver in the healthcare industry. This method of driving traffic allows us to leverage other people's audiences to build our own. It is the classic networking and referral tool that sometimes gets lost in all the social components of communication today. If you are a small-town, Naturopathic Doctor with a focus on women in their thirties, why not reach out and link up with a local yoga studio? If you can provide a high value of healthcare to those already looking to become healthier, find out where else your audience hangs out and put yourself there. In return, you can refer your own patients to the yoga studio if that's something that fits well into their transformational health plan. Similarly, online, reciprocal relationships with people who have complimentary audiences to your own are a great place to deliver a webinar or 'live' content on someone else's platform. Relationship traffic is a win-win for everyone involved, including your respective audiences.

It is worth noting that I did not reference referrals as a traffic source for your practice. While referrals represent one of the highest quality leads into your business, they are equally unreliable in their predictability. Managing your referrals like gold is a critical business strategy, but it will not build your business with the reliability you will need.

THE SIGNATURE TALK

The first time I delivered my Signature Talk was to a room of two hundred people at a Crohn's and Colitis Association meeting. I had given talks for them before, but I had not tested out my new format. My high school background in theatre had me wanting to engage them more deeply on an emotional level. My fellow speakers were well credentialled, but they were 'by the book', working to prove how much they knew and not necessarily trying their skills at engaging the crowd.

My talk opened with six provocative words: 'How many of you drink milk'? A quarter of the hands went up. 'How many of you were told by your physician that your diet does not influence your disease'? Three-quarters of the hands went up. 'How many of you experienced a lessening of your symptoms when you removed milk from your diet'? The entire room raised their hands. 'Well, today, I am going to share with you even more strategies to mitigate your symptoms, expedite your journey to healing and take back control of your health'. The room was on the edge of their seats. I had challenged the status quo. I acquired fifteen new patients that day but was never asked to speak for this organization again. My talk served my audience but not the traditionally minded physicians and board members in the back row.

Driving people to your social channel or website is an important first step, but how do you move them even deeper into your business ecosystem? Of all the lead magnets and tactics that can be deployed, the Signature Talk is my favourite tool to teach, convert and demonstrate your value in real time. The Signature Talk can be delivered on a community stage, a webinar or even on a podcast. The structure is designed to be modular and shortened as needed. Once your Arena of Authority has been established, crafting a single Signature Talk enables you to have a reliable and measurable strategy to invite people to book. It's an opportunity for you to start undoing some of the thinking that has led them into the lifestyle that drove them to your lead magnet—your Google or Facebook ad or your Instagram Live—in the first place. It reinforces their problem now and is an opportunity for you to give them a clear call to action.

The Signature Talk is one of the most critical ingredients in your arsenal of marketing. While this overview will get you started, going in deep will be instrumental to your success. Deeper trainings and overviews are available at impactmedicinebook.com /resources.

THE SIGNATURE TALK

INTRODUCTION

1—HOOK

2—CREDENTIAL

3—OPEN STORY

4—SOCIAL PROOF

5—TIME

6—OUTCOME

THE ONE THING

WHAT IS THE ONE THING THAT YOU WANT PEOPLE TO LEARN FROM THIS WEBINAR?

WHAT PROBLEM ARE YOU SOLVING FOR THEM?

E.G., HOW TO BUILD A PROFITABLE BUSINESS

DECONSTRUCTION

1—NEW WAY OF VIEWING THE PROBLEM #1
THE MOST IMPORTANT INVESTMENT IN YOUR BUSINESS IS THE ONE THAT MOVES YOU TOWARD PREDICTABLE PROFITABILITY THE FASTEST.

2—NEW WAY OF VIEWING THE PROBLEM #2
DEFINE 3 KEY PERFORMANCE INDICATORS THAT WILL ASSIST YOU IN MONITORING YOUR PROGRESS TOWARD PROFITABILITY.

3—NEW WAY OF VIEWING THE PROBLEM #3
THE CHALLENGES YOU HAVE FACED UP UNTIL NOW ARE NOT YOUR FAULT, BUT FIXING THEM IS YOUR RESPONSIBILITY.

RECONSTRUCTION

1—US VS. THEM
E.G., (THEY ARE GOING TO TELL YOU TO BE EVERYWHERE, SPEND ALL YOUR TIME ON SOCIAL, WE DON'T THINK YOUR SOCIAL MEDIA FOLLOWING HAS ANYTHING TO DO WITH BUSINESS SUCCESS)

2—NEW FACT
A "REAL" BUSINESS REQUIRES RECURRENT, PREDICTABLE REVENUE, MONTH AFTER MONTH, YEAR AFTER YEAR. THIS WILL NOT BE ACHIEVED THROUGH A SOCIAL MEDIA FOLLOWING

3—YOU WERE NEVER TOLD THE TRUTH
NOT HAVING THIS STRUCTURE IS NOT YOUR FAULT. NO ONE EVER TOLD YOU THAT THIS WAS THE FIRST AND MOST IMPORTANT BENCHMARK IN BUILDING A SUCCESSFUL BUSINESS.

INDOCTRINATION

1—PROVIDE THE THEORY BEHIND DECONSTRUCTION ITEM 1.

PROVIDE THE THEORY BEHIND A NEW WAY OF THINKING.

2—PROVIDE THE THEORY BEHIND DECONSTRUCTION ITEM 2.

PROVIDE THE THEORY BEHIND A NEW WAY OF THINKING.

3—PROVIDE THE THEORY BEHIND DECONSTRUCTION ITEM 3.

PROVIDE THE THEORY BEHIND A NEW WAY OF THINKING.

CLOSE & CTA

1—OBJECTIONS

2—CLOSE THE STORY LOOP

3—HIGHLIGHT THE HERO'S EPIPHANY

4—THE CTA

Figure 10: The Signature Talk. This is a framework and roadmap to delivering a consistent, action-inspiring presentation.

The Introduction

This Signature Talk roadmap lays out a clear format in five phases starting with the introduction. Your introduction should contain five main points: (1) a hook, (2) a relatable story, (3) social proof or case study, (4) the length of the talk and (5) credentials. From there, transition to the next phase, Deconstruction. All of this will come to life for you in our online training and resources (impactmedi cinebook.com/resources).

Deconstruction

In the Deconstruction phase, you are literally deconstructing the way of thinking (often conventional advice) that is keeping people stuck with respect to their health. This is where you get to undo the commonly held beliefs that are preventing your audience from taking action. For the Deconstruction phase to be most effective, you will want to challenge your audience and trigger them emotionally. Don't be afraid to say something provocative: 'If you have been told that the birth control pill will solve all of your problems, you have been given bad advice'.

The Deconstruction phase breaks down all the reasons why their beliefs aren't 100 per cent accurate and opens the door to a new way of thinking. Deconstruction casts doubt in the beliefs holding people back and opens their minds to a new solution, which is taught in the next phase.

Teaching

To be clear, the Teaching phase is not a comprehensive overview of your formal education. This part of your Signature Talk comprises no more than a quarter of the entire presentation. You aren't packing years of teachings into one talk. In this phase, your job is to highlight the key teaching points that support your Deconstruction claims. You can start by telling that patient with heart disease how their diet actually influences the progression of their problem or the woman on birth control how to control the cause of her PCOS if she hopes to resolve the problem in the future. The Teaching phase further engages your patient with the science and theory that supports your Deconstruction claims and consolidates the science.

Reconstruction

In this phase, the patient's prior beliefs, now in question, are replaced, and a reconstructed version of beliefs is introduced. This is where you show people that there is a more empowering and transformational way of thinking about the topic and possibly their challenge, and it is a consolidation of the Teaching you just completed. The Reconstruction phase is a concise rebuilding of the thinking that will support the audience's opportunity to work deeper with you directly.

Close

The final phase is the Close, where you present the patient with a clear call to action. What is it that they should be doing after viewing the Signature Talk? Do you want them to schedule a Discovery call with your office? Or take another action that moves them further along in your process? Bridging the Deconstruction and moving them towards the opportunity to work with you is a process that takes practice, but it is well worth the investment of time and courage.

CONVERSION TOOL

The Signature Talk is such a critical tool because it serves as both a lead magnet and a conversion tool into your practice or onto your mailing list. Traffic and the subsequent conversion are the Holy Grail of digital marketing. Moving people from 'thinking about it' to actually booking an appointment is critical to building your practice. If people don't book directly from a Signature Talk, there is a tried-and-true tactic that moves people from curious to committed—the Discovery call.

THE DISCOVERY CALL

Once a person decides they want to speak with you further about permanently changing their health, you have an option to include access to a 'meet and greet' opportunity, frequently called a Discovery call. While this used to happen in person, virtual care platforms afford you the opportunity and the efficiency of delivering this call online. This is an opportunity to showcase your services or, as you get deeper into your career, interview prospective clients to make sure the desire to move forward is reciprocal.

While many busy practitioners chose to forgo the 'meet and greet' experience over time, I used it as a valuable opportunity to make sure I wasn't getting myself into a relationship that I didn't want long term. This step is not a mandatory element of your process, but you may find it saves you time and energy over the long term. Over my fifteen years of practice, I developed a process that enabled me to be efficient and effective in how I delivered a Discovery call or 'meet and greet' experience. I called this approach 'The Seven Ps to Prospect a Patient'.

1. **Position.** Contextualize the call/appointment. Let the person know what to expect and the timeline. 'Hi, Mary. I'm excited to have the opportunity to speak with you over the next fifteen minutes to discuss what's going on and how I might be able to help you'. I've told her what's going to happen without making the mistake of saying I can fix her issue on the call today.

2. **People.** Understand that there are two people in the relationship. You will want to understand what you can do to help the patient but also find out why they came to you. What was it specifically that drew them to this Discovery call? Look for gaps between what they need and what you are offering to see if you are the right fit.

3. **Pinpoint the Problem.** Assess, don't impress. Figure out what's going on and what needs to happen to resolve the problem. Don't belittle the person or the information they found coming into this call. If another practitioner told them something you don't agree with, don't speak negatively about it. You're not here to pull down others,

but to assess the person's issue. Your response should be something like, 'Based on my experience and what you are telling me, this is what I think'. (Yes, we all know you need/want to provide a comprehensive intake, but let's be honest, you probably have a theory about what is going on. Share your theory and let them know that the intake will confirm or deny your suspicions.)

4. **Process.** Transition from 'you are stuck because' to 'the process is'. Fill the gap the person is having. Let them know what the process will be like working with you. Introduce outcomes and milestones, not appointment length and cost. 'Mary, I suspect you are not seeing progress because the medication you are taking is not treating the cause of the problem. Working together, we will move you through three phases of care that will address the underlying cause of your discomfort'.

5. **Proof.** Show commonalities in the person's struggle. 'Can I tell you a story'? Open up the person's mind to let them know that you have resolved the challenge of a patient with similar issues before.

6. **Pudding.** Now that the person is feeling good and having hope that you can resolve their issue, it's nice to leave them with a win for the day. If openings in your schedule won't allow you to see the person for several weeks, it could be depleting. Give them a win. Lean in to that heightened state of dopamine. Tell them something that they can do to get started on a road to recovery *today*.

7. **Planning.** Plan the process moving forward. Don't hand over the person to a secretary or some online booking platform. Do this yourself. Ask, 'When can we get you on the calendar'? This is also the phase where you provide an overview of the cost and other follow-up logistics. Don't belabour these details. Be direct and ask if they have their calendar with them to take the next step.

This traffic strategy isn't something we learned in our eight thousand years of schooling, and it will evolve, in detail over time. Your traffic and conversion strategy will differ from your colleagues' based on your location, skills, niche and metrics. The most important element is that you move forward with a process you can measure and deploy with confidence.

CHECK-IN

1. Do I have a reliable traffic strategy in my practice?
2. Build a Signature Talk that you can use on other people's platforms or deliver to your own audience.
3. Find ten people online or in your community with a complimentary audience to yours. Identify how you could provide value for them and reach out about having them on your platform to start!

CHAPTER 17

THE IMPACT MARKETING SYSTEM

These Discovery calls and social media strategies didn't all come to me the day I opened the doors to my practice. My marketing system wasn't handed to me like a gift with a big red bow on top. I developed it through trial and error, and it took time. That first Signature Talk, the one where I offended all of the high-profile doctors in the room, was the start of my refinement of my marketing system. Through years of trials and tribulations, I have deployed versions of my Signature Talk and the subsequent system of nurture to sell millions of dollars in transformations.

There are coaches and trainers all over the internet who sell their courses and systems with claims such as, 'I've spent hundreds of thousands of dollars trying to figure out the perfect system, and now I'm sharing it with you'. Some of those ads are hard to believe, but that's exactly what happened to me. Before I started actually seeing some traction with my approach, I had no idea how to sell. I had no idea how to move people to act on a Discovery call. I was trying everything, and things worked or failed for no particular reason.

I was using the right pieces. I tried social media strategies. I tried webinars. I tried building a brand around what I was selling. I tried it all, and they were all the things I had been learning were the right things to do. The problem was that I didn't have them in the proper order.

Practitioners see patients with the same things, but with a different flavour. You've heard it, right? *'I've tried everything, and nothing works: every cleanse, every diet, every medication, treatment and exercise. None of it works for me'.* After you settle them down and look into everything they have been trying, you realize that they *have* been taking some quality measures. The problem is that they have been doing all of these things at once, with no strategy, consistency and definitely no sequence. They were doing many of the right things but in the wrong order or frequency.

THE IMPACT MARKETING SYSTEM

TRAFFIC
(PAID) TRAFFIC
SOCIAL MEDIA
OTHER'S AUDIENCE
REFERRALS

Landing page/website
PLATFORM

OPT-IN PAGE
Collect their contact
information in exchange
for something valuable

01

02
**NURTURE
SEQUENCE & CTA**
Add early value

EDUCATIONAL TOOL
Webinar/Signature
Talk/Challenge

03

04
CALL TO ACTION
Tell them what you
want them to do next

DISCOVERY CALL
Gateway to 1:1 care or
high-priced option

**FOUNDATIONAL
PROGRAM**
If they are not intere-
sted or ready for 1:1
care, downhill to
Foundational Program

Figure 11: The IMPACT Marketing system. This diagram illustrates where all of the marketing tactics we have been discussing come together as a single marketing strategy. More resources and support related to the IMPACT Marketing System can be found at impactmedicinebook.com/resources.

For practitioners struggling with these marketing strategies, thinking, *I've tried everything*, you're really just lacking a system. You are trying to utilize all these tools at once instead of putting them into a functioning order. This was the mistake I made early on, and it's one I have learned from. It's how I came to create the marketing strategy that has worked for so many clients. Now I help providers find their authority, attract their patients and build their businesses, so they can transform people's health and their lives, while transforming themselves and their careers in the process.

BONUS: EMAIL MARKETING TACTICS

Everything that we have done leading up to this point has been to drive the right people to the right offer. From there, we need to nurture that person into realizing that we can solve their problem and that we are the best person for the job. They need to be consistently reminded that we have the solution they seek. Our marketing copy has to relay that position.

If you are using the Traffic Trifecta properly—meaning you are utilizing at least two of the three traffic strategies at any given time—you should be driving people to your lead magnets, Signature Talk, or directly to your booking link. As your email list grows from these opt-in offers, you now have the responsibility to nurture these people through email to help engender trust, pinpoint their challenge and leave them feeling confident that you are the right person to help solve their problem. An email marketing strategy that doesn't deliver consistent emails is not worth the effort. Yes, of course, you will lose people each time you email. But don't think of this as a rejection of you and your offer; think of it as a refinement of your audience. You're not doing a good thing for your business by simply putting up landing pages and collecting emails. You need to be driving them to move further along in the process.

So, what exactly should you include in your email nurture sequence—this string of emails that are triggered when someone first opts into your list? Here is a cursory overview of what you can consider including.

Email #1

The first email should be pushed out as soon as the person opts in to your lead magnet and should contain exactly what you promised. Is it an informational PDF? The link to a video? An e-book? Whatever it is, send it to them immediately. Also, let them know that a series of emails is coming their way. Let them know the schedule of each and the intention behind these emails, which is to dive deeper into the information the person is seeking.

Email #2

Identify and label their pain point in the way the person on the other end sees it, not the way *you* see it—not in medical terms. Then give basic tips to help. Don't give away the entire cure, but do make sure you give them something that will result in incremental improvement.

Email #3

Underscore the pain point again and talk about your solution. This is a great place to introduce your story, your 'why' and a little bit about yourself. Remember, people don't like to read. Keep any conversation about you interesting and not delivered in sweeping paragraphs. By the third email, you also want to ensure that you are providing a clear call to action about how to move forward and work with you ditrectly.

Email #4

Reiterate the pain point and the solution and add some proof about your claims. Add case studies, or even better, add a testimonial or two to the bottom of the email. Up to this point, all the information has been coming from you. Now, let them hear from others—let the social proof do the talking. If your regulations prohibit testimonials, opt for a brief, brief, *brief* case study instead.

Email #5

This email should focus on life beyond the problem. This can include another case study or just generally speak about what clients are able to do—the enhancements they are able to make in their daily lives—after working with you. Focus on the outcomes people are realizing as a result of your process.

Add a Call to Action (CTA)

Starting with email #2, you can start sending out calls to action. 'Here's your pain point, here's how the solution goes, and here's the plan for this email series. Listen, some people like to hop right to the front of the line and start getting to the root of their problem. If you fall into that category, here's how to do it'. If they want to get right to the point, don't make them wait around until the end of the email campaign.

Add a PS

In many cases, this could be your most important, personal piece. I never pass up an opportunity to add a PS to the end of an email. After the call to action, I'll add a PS that says something like, 'PS, have you tried sitting like this to avoid your back pain?' Or, 'PS, If you aren't finding these emails helpful yet and you just want to get on a call, here's my number. Give me a call'.

As with everything in this book, this is a framework and not a rule. You don't need to limit your emails to a total of five. You can have more, or you can have less. You don't need to drive people to a Discovery call if you feel more comfortable bringing them into your office instead. What's important to do, though, is to monitor what is working and what isn't.

MANAGING THE METRICS

There's a lot involved in deploying a marketing strategy. For this reason, many people fail to track the results of each piece or the system as a whole. This is one of the reasons many strategies fail to produce the desired results. You aren't sure what's working and what isn't, and if you continue to spend time and energy pursuing resources that aren't driving the outcomes you want, your morale becomes depleted. You become the patient that walks into your office saying, 'I've tried everything'.

Here are some metrics to consider monitoring.

New Leads

Your new leads are the new people that you've put onto your mailing list. These people come down your marketing pipeline, starting at the first point of contact, and they should always be added to your mailing list.

Show-Up Rate

This is the number of people who actually show up to an event such as a webinar or talk. If your goal is to drive people to a webinar, this is the number of people who actually attended, the percentage, compared to the number who signed up to *say* they would attend.

Conversion from your Lead Tool

These conversions are the number of people (or the percentage of people) who moved from your lead magnet, webinar or whatever tool you're using onto the next step. These are the people who actually took the next step in your funnel—for example, booking a Discovery call or initial appointment. You will want to track conversions at every step along your funnel.

Conversion from Discovery Call

How many people bought a product because of your Discovery call? And if you're selling more than one product, you will want to look at this number for each one.

Retention

How long are people sticking with you? This isn't for products or offerings that are one-time use. This is geared towards the lifetime value of a given patient and whether or not you are able to retain them with the process at-hand.

For email marketing, there are additional metrics to look into. They are specific to email campaigns and can be viewed for each one within your campaign. Your open rate, click-through rate, hits to your landing page, conversions, and new subscriber numbers will all be important metrics to look into.

With email marketing, you have many tools from which to choose, and some are free. Each one has metrics automatically built into each email you send out, so there is no manual process behind finding these numbers. All you need to do is review the numbers, pay attention to what's working best and pivot your email strategy accordingly—the same way you would leverage blood work to pivot your treatment plan.

I use these strategies and tools in my business. I deploy this type of system to the practitioners in my mastermind group. Once they have a system in place and start tracking the numbers, they can make decisions about what to do next. The metrics guide them towards what's working and inform their decisions around what needs to change.

CHECK-IN

1. Do I have a system to attract new leads into my practice?
2. Of the marketing efforts I have tried, what has worked best, and why?
3. Take a few minutes to draw out a marketing funnel for your ideal client. Include the initial source of traffic, the

opt-in tool, conversion tool and content overview for your nurture sequence.

4. Visit impactmedicinebook.com/resources for a checklist on what to look for in an email marketing system.

PART FOUR: ATTRACTION—KEY TAKEAWAYS

Feel confident that, although you may hear about varied marketing tactics and strategies from other sources, you now have a place you can come back to and fit those strategies into a distinct system—a framework or tool for attraction that also improves people's health.

Marketing, branding and even creating a clinical process can be fun sides of building a practice. But what, really, is the point of all of this? Yes, I know you want to impact people's health, but as a business, it is critical that you are also driving revenue and income into your practice and life. In the next section, we will be addressing the fundamentals of business finance, money mindset and the benchmarks your marketing efforts and offerings should be aiming to support.

For more IMPACT Medicine resources, visit
impactmedicinebook.com/resources.

PART FIVE

CENTS AND SENSE

'Money isn't the most important thing in life,
but it's reasonably close to oxygen
on the 'gotta have it' scale'.

—Zig Ziglar

hen good people make good money, they can do good things. This is how I choose to view life, entrepreneurship and a financially strong practice or business. This view isn't a symptom of toxic positivity; it is a decision I have made in response to the world around me and the endless examples of callous capitalism and entrepreneurial greed. Balanced with this negative narrative and the nefarious stories of dubious pursuits of wealth are countless examples of entrepreneurs and innovators who are putting their financial security to good use.

So much of the story we write as adults is influenced by the script we find ourselves within as children. My parents had a massive influence on my life and how I make decisions. My mother inspired my curiosity around healing. She had shelves of books around the house that touched on healing and psychology, and they drew me in. She definitely piqued that curiosity in me that led to my interest in Naturopathic Medicine and underscored a prioritization around health and prevention.

My father influenced prevention and health through a different lens—the mechanics and importance of discussing and knowing how to manage money. I had always seen my dad's business. As the only child of divorced parents, I frequently found myself colouring in his office or photocopying my hands with the ladies at the front desk. I saw when business was stressful, and I experienced the delight when there were wins and upticks in the business's success. This transparency was equally shared at home. We talked about the stock market, and I was charged pretend interest for the candy money I would borrow when we went to the store. When I was around twelve and able to finally form some sort of financial insight without regurgitating his ideas, my dad handed me a book, *The Richest Man in Babylon* by George S. Clason. I was given one week to read it and report on my findings. One week later, perched on the deck of our cabin, I shared my perspective on the book. My dad knew I had read it and had understood the essence of the book—*pay yourself first*. He promptly handed me a crisp $100-bill and announced a small increase in my allowance. He then handed me book number two, *One Up on Wall Street* by Peter Lynch. He gave me a month to get through it—the stakes were getting higher.

Every few months, a new book would come my way. My dad felt strongly that school would do little to advance my financial education, and as a woman, society would overlook my potential competence and interest in the subject. As my knowledge increased, so too did the breadth of my exposure. Soon after my introduction to Peter Lynch, my dad and I started buying shares of stock in companies I liked—Disney, Gap—and every morning, I would run downstairs, open the newspaper and look to see how my stocks were doing. I watched as world events, supply chains and inflation influenced my picks. Not unlike the physiological systems that influence the body and health, I was learning to appreciate the systemic influences that impacted money and future wealth. My future self would come to benefit equally from my early exposure to both health and wealth knowledge accumulation.

The parallels between money and health are something we have to acknowledge. You cannot be a practitioner who embraces overall health but doesn't strive to do the same with wealth. As I tracked the categories of stress that most impacted my patients, health and finances were the leading triggers and causes of their chronic stress. So, how can we, as root-cause practitioners, favour one trigger while overlooking the others ourselves?

I know this idea of finance isn't one everyone was brought up to respect or even acknowledge. I know that money was often the source of great strife, tension and pain in many upbringings. I also know that leaning into the study of health and the action of helping others was a direct response to the discomfort and inadequacy that was triggered in response to people's financial situations. And yet, despite this, I am going to invite you to write an updated version to your financial testament. As the author of your entrepreneurial journey, you get to write the ending. You get the final word.

For many of us, women especially (thanks, society), the idea of having open and honest talks about finances can be tough. It can make you feel lost or out of place. But the faster you get comfortable talking about money, the more you can begin to leverage it. This section will discuss the reasons why we need to normalize the process of talking about money and what we can do to improve our financial situations in our personal and business lives.

CHAPTER 18

RISK AND REWARD

There is something you need to know about business and money. Money will optimally flow in the direction of the person or people taking the biggest risk.

Between my second and third baby, I had a brief stint as the CEO of a digital health media company that connects health-seeking consumers to practitioners like you. I started in this role when my second daughter was ten weeks old and two years before I was pregnant with my third child. I was working like a dog and leveraging every ounce of skill and energy I could muster. But that didn't mean I was getting paid. Because, well, that's what happens with a startup. You invest what you can, and in the beginning, it is time.

At each stage of your business development, you have different currencies you can offer the equation of growth. In the beginning, it is time, then money, then relationships and finally expertise. As you get started and are working hard to get ahead, it will feel like you are carrying the brunt of the load and taking new risks every day. But when it comes to business, your emotional risks don't factor into the equation.

It's important to note that risk comes in two forms: emotional and financial. Emotional risk will be variable among us and often involves putting yourself out there on social media or speaking publicly. This is less about working hard and more about tackling hard situations. Emotional risks can be low or high, but that determination is based on the individual, not the task. Financial risk, in contrast, is more clear-cut. It is not about who works harder; it is about who has to stick their neck out the furthest. It may feel unfair to hand over 40 per cent of what you make to a clinic owner, but they are the ones footing the bills for rent, insurance, hydro and staff... regardless of whether you see patients. They are the ones holding the greatest degree of risk.

Collectively, as practitioners, we have taken a huge personal risk. We have spent eight years in school and amassed hundreds of thousands of dollars in debt for our educations. We passed up income opportunities in our twenties so that we could pursue this system of education. As a practitioner, you put forward a massive amount of risk to get where you are, but if you don't recoup that choice with your split, you regain it in your fees.

Risk is part of adult life. For us as practitioners, we place this huge financial cloud over our heads to become licenced. Eight in ten physicians in North America incur debt to complete any type of medical school. And 18 per cent will borrow more than $300,000. As an example, for Naturopathic Doctors in North America, the average student debt is greater than $150,000. Compare that to the average income of around $85,000.[10] And that's money to live off of, not just to pay back. In contrast, a plumber who works every working day of the year—261 days—earns well over $100,000 annually. This reality doesn't undermine the value of the work the plumber completes; it underscores the need for you to fully understand how regulation, education and responsibility drive the cost of your time even higher.

This inequality in pay is overlooked by practitioners who have become accustomed to living in debt and who are frequently conditioned to believe that finances are the largest barrier to people accessing care. For many, coming out of school where they were living off of student loans, going into further debt to open a practice isn't a big deal—it's part of the process.

The thoughts surrounding this idea and pay structure need to be addressed. And that's not just an opinion. It's based on these facts. The sustainability of the entire allied health industry is predicated upon it. Without change, the future for practitioners is financially unsustainable. Becoming a practitioner is not a guarantee of financial success. Who would have thought that the risk and financial reward to become a practitioner would be so disproportionate to the effort and cost of the education required to practice?

There are huge secondary implications to this as well. When we move people into careers that have a very poor return on financial

---

10   The Association of Accredited Naturopathic Medical Colleges (AANMC), 2020 Graduate Success and Compensation Study (Washington, DC: AANMC, 2020), https://aanmc.org/wp-content/uploads/2020/06/2020-Graduate -Success-and-Compensation-Study.pdf.

investment, we self-select people who have the luxury of not worrying about their finances, whether that be people who are supported by spouses or have other sources of income. And when we start to self-select for financial stability, we limit the diversity of those who can practice our systems of care and, in turn, the spectrum of patients who will access it.

Cents and Sense is about more than generating higher earnings for practitioners. It's about disrupting the whole system. It is about paying people appropriately for their time and designing a compensation model that matches the risks we took and the expertise we acquired.

THE COST OF CARE

As a highly educated practitioner, it is important that you understand that seeing patients one-to-one is the single most expensive way to deliver healthcare. Your time and ability to deliver health strategy are extremely valuable. In fact, the more experience you possess and the more refined your skill, the more valuable your time becomes. While this may be obvious, what does not translate well is how your experience and the value of your skills translates into your fee schedule or financial model.

You do not sell your time; you sell your strategy.

This single differentiation in perspective is the difference between those who find opportunities for leverage and those who get stuck trading their time for money, forever.

In the next chapter, we're getting into a strategy for structuring your fees. But, before we talk pricing, let's further break down the expenses and value that inform your fees.

For a long time, the way that practitioners set their fees was with their gut. They/we looked around at what others were charging and smacked ours right in the middle. We settled on a number that either 'felt right' or was selected by a clinic owner on our behalf. In either scenario, the fees neglected to acknowledge the actual cost of delivering the care, and it simplified our thinking when it came to innovating ways to make our care more accessible financially. These are costs that inform your fees—and the list is not exhaustive; there are many more.

Physical overhead. This might be the cost of rent, hydro and utilities, or it may be the split you give back to a clinic to utilize their space.

Health and safety requirements and inefficiencies. There is usually a cost of your time or money to maintain your required health and safety standards.

Cost of acquisition of new clients. The cost in terms of time and money to advertise to consistently acquire new clients.

Cost of your education. This goes without saying, but this also needs to account for the delay in your earning years due to the time you spent in school.

Cost to maintain your licence. This annual cost must be accounted for in your annual operating budget.

Cost of CE requirements. This will be an ongoing cost, but it is also something that adds to your ongoing value as a practitioner.

The level of risk you incur (both financial and procedural). This right here is why you can charge more for your time than a plumber—you have more professional responsibility. Also, if you are a clinic owner or if you have associates working under your brand, you again have more financial and reputational responsibility. This too favours you financially.

The opportunity cost of your time seeing patients. The cost refers to the loss you potentially incur because you could be doing something more financially fruitful with your time (e.g. washing the bathrooms in your clinic versus using that time to see more patients). There is an 'opportunity cost' to cleaning versus working at your highest earning capacity.

The toll on your health. Yes, this factors into your value.

The outcome you promise. This, more than years in practice or the letters behind your name, drives the value of your time and offering.

Your demand. As with outcome, as the demand for your expertise goes up, so too does your pricing.

The perception of value you cultivate. While you never want to lower your fees for the purposes of marketing, you can increase them to set a heightened perception of value, especially when it is accompanied by a well-presented brand.

Your niche and Arena of Authority. Not all niches are created equal. Part of your fees are determined by what people with a particular problem will be willing to pay for your solution.

Do you see now why you can't just drop your fees somewhere in the middle of what others are offering? Equally important is having a conversation with potential clinic owners about how you want to structure your fees.

Before we delve into the mechanics of money and your fees, we need to return, one more time, to the first section of the book, Intention. Without knowing what you want to earn and how you want to live, evaluating some of the factors I cited above will be difficult to contextualize.

Far too many practitioners throw up their hands when it comes to deciding what they want financially. 'I just want to help people' becomes the default mindset, but even that requires a more nuanced approach. As you have seen, your fee structure is informed by more than your emotions, and so too is your approach to making care financially accessible for more people. This is the last concept we tackle before we set your fees and lay the foundation of financial literacy.

SETTING THE STAGE FOR A
BETTER SOLUTION

Reaching more people requires that we innovate our offer, not simply lower our fees. We have already established that one-to-one care is expensive. While you may want to drop the price to make your offer easier to access, you still need to account for the cost of care delivery. Reaching more people does not happen by lowering your prices; it happens by innovating your offer.

By leveraging the Quadrants of Care, we can serve more patients, at various stages of readiness, without sacrificing the cost or one-to-one visits. Additionally, you add the bonus of income diversification, which further reduces your risk as a business owner. This is a 'cake and eat it too' scenario. We can reach more people in less time, satisfy more patients at the level they're seeking, make more money and, as clinician entrepreneurs, scale our businesses and time.

The reward for this isn't only financial; it allows an entire lifestyle change for you, the practitioner. You have more time for your kids, your partner, your friends and your adventures. Changing how you charge for services alleviates stress. The excitement you felt when you stepped into this profession returns, and you feel empowered to fully show up, knowing that all the risk you are taking is worth it because you are finally enjoying the full reward.

CHECK-IN

1. Clearly identify what you want to be earning personally and within your business on an annual basis.
2. List the financial risk/debt and exposure you are currently managing personally and professionally.
3. Identify where you may be paying a high price when it comes to opportunity cost. For example, do you need a VA? What would the revenue look like if you spent that time seeing more patients or creating content instead?

CHAPTER 19

SIMPLE FINANCIAL LITERACY FOR CLINICIAN ENTREPRENEURS

My dad wasn't the only family member with whom I spoke about money. My grandmother and I used to get together on Sunday afternoons and talk about business, women's rights and, begrudgingly, politics. Born in 1921, when women typically didn't own businesses or manage their finances, my grandmother was a bit different. She liked to brag about how she didn't have her first kid until she was thirty because she wanted to travel the world.

She eventually met the man who would become my grandfather. He wasn't very open to the idea of his wife making her own money, nor was he overly generous in what he doled out for her extraneous spending. My grandmother, a natural entrepreneur, didn't need her man to provide. She devised a plan instead. She convinced my grandfather that she could 'handle' a small little laundromat on the main street of town. It would provide a little bit of extra money, and it wouldn't require a lot of work. He agreed. My grandmother knew this type of business would be cash-based, which meant that her husband wouldn't know exactly how much money was being generated.

Many years later, as my mother was helping to clean out my grandparents' garage, she bent down to lift up a bucket from the floor—and nearly threw out her back. She lifted the rags that had been stuffed in the bucket and, to her surprise, found thousands of quarters. Surveying the room, she noticed more buckets filled with coins. It was like finding a long-lost treasure. In all those years of operating that business, my grandmother had enjoyed a steady revenue stream and had even squirrelled away a hefty savings in those buckets.

My grandmother was the first woman to really talk to me about money. She told me that I needed to prioritize my money and, more importantly, to have my own. She said that having my own money would empower me to sustain myself without ever having to depend on someone else. I valued her independence, self-sufficiency and unapologetic ability to serve others and herself at the same time.

Later in her life, she and my grandfather divorced. She opened several more businesses and enjoyed her independence—financial and otherwise. My grandmother used her money however she pleased, including making donations to the church and her favourite charities.

When good people make good money, they can do good things.

THE PEOPLE TO KNOW

Patients come to us to solve their healthcare challenges. If they have complex issues that they cannot resolve on their own, they know they can turn to us to help find a solution. We need to carry that same mindset into business ownership. Even if you're 'not a numbers person', you still have the skills to do what's necessary to keep your business finances in order.

When it comes to money, many practitioners try to manage it on their own. Don't. Wary of sharing their financial details or spending anything, they avoid hiring an expert. A business owner must keep accurate records, and as a clinician entrepreneur, you are a business owner. If you're audited by the government and your financial records are not in order, you could be fined, or worse.

Most of us don't have the acumen needed to keep those tight financial records. (Full disclosure, even though my dad and grandmother talked to me about money, and I had a genuine interest in finance, I had zero interest or skill in managing my own financial records.) Managing this piece of your business is not just about avoiding financial repercussions; it is about the opportunity cost of your time and the savings that come from allocating and 'writing things off' accordingly.

When you commit to growing your practice, two people will make your financial situation much easier: a bookkeeper and an accountant.

Your Bookkeeper

If you add just one person to your team, make it a bookkeeper. This is the record keeper of your business. Your bookkeeper knows how much it costs to operate your business, itemizing every expense and maintaining all the necessary documents to ensure your finances are in order and you're in good shape in the event of an audit and your annual tax submission.

Some practitioners and other business owners take care of their own bookkeeping, claiming they want to 'get familiar with the numbers'. There are two problems with this. First, as a business owner, you don't have time! The opportunity cost is too high. You have too much else on your plate to add 'bookkeeper' to your job description. Second, saying you want to take care of your own books to learn the numbers is like saying you want to perform your own open-heart surgery so that you can get familiar with your cardiovascular system. It is not a good strategy.

An important distinction to remember about your bookkeeper is that they focus on the past. They do not necessarily help you plan for the future. When it comes to future finances, the business owner, CEO and/or clinician entrepreneur—I'm looking at you—needs to be in charge. Your bookkeeper is not in charge of financial strategy. They meticulously manage all the financial details and records regarding transactions within your business.

Your Accountant

Your accountant is your communicator between your business's financial records and the government. Their job is to take the bookkeeper's records and submit the final book report, if you will, to the government. It's their job to understand the interplay between your personal and business finances, then record and acknowledge money in each with the greatest degree of efficiency. Over time, as your business becomes more sophisticated, so too will that responsibility. Your accountant must take on a higher understanding of tax strategies and other specialized areas.

When business owners first look into hiring an accountant, there's often a negative stigma associated with the upfront cost. This is probably no different than that sticker shock our patients experience when we first ask them to invest in their health. But these costs are far less than the fees and taxes you would have to pay in the end if you didn't have this expert at your side. Accountants mitigate the risk of future taxes because they understand small business finance and know how to leverage personal and business finances against one another. They help you save money, which you can then reinvest in your business and marketing strategies.

You don't need to hire the top accounting firm in the country to handle your business. All you need is someone who understands your industry and puts you in the best possible position financially.

THE BASICS

You do not have to become a financial expert to maintain a financially stable business, but you should take it upon yourself to learn the basics, so you can have productive conversations with your bookkeeper and accountant and make informed decisions based on their records.

Terminology

I'm not a finance major, but I am financially savvy enough to give you the clinician entrepreneur's high-level, meaningful version of terms you need to know to run your business.

- **Income.** Income is a catch-all term for incoming money, used interchangeably with 'revenue'.
- **Revenue.** Revenue is incoming money. There are two types:
  - ▷ *Gross Revenue* is all the revenue your business generates before anything is taken out. A business can have $10 million in gross revenue, but if their operating expenses are $9.9 million, they have just $100,000 in the more important net revenue.
  - ▷ *Net Revenue* is what's left over after you subtract all of your operating expenses from your sales. This is the final number after you subtract all of your expenses. When having a conversation about revenue, it's important to know whether the number being discussed is gross or net revenue.
- **Profit.** This is the money left over after you subtract your expenses *and* your personal income—your salary. So, gross revenue is all the money generated, net revenue is gross revenue minus expenses, and profit is net revenue minus whatever you pay yourself.
- **Expenses.** This is the cost to run your business. For the purposes of this cursory overview, there are two types of expenses: *Fixed* and *Operational*.

▷ *Fixed Expenses.* Fixed expenses are your monthly, guaranteed expenses. These are things that won't change, no matter what's happening within your business. Rent, for example, will always remain constant, whether you have one hundred patients or just one.

▷ *Operational Expenses.* Operational expenses can fluctuate, and you have more control over how much they go up or down from month to month. Your electronic health record software, for instance, is an operational expense. Contractor fees are operational expenses. These are the expenses that you need to operate your business month to month.

▸ **COGS (Cost of Goods Sold).** COGS is included in your operational expenses. If you're selling products, this is what you paid for the products that you're selling. If you paid $7 for a bottle of supplements and you sell them for $10, your COGS is $7, and your profit is $3. From an accounting perspective, COGS doesn't include labour activities—only the cost of physical products.

Statements

Your bookkeeper and accountant handle a number of statements that show how your business is doing financially on any given month or quarter. Understanding these statements allows you to determine best next steps.

- **Profit and Loss Statement (a.k.a. Income Statement).** Your profit and loss, or P&L, statement summarizes the revenue, costs and expenses incurred during a specific period of time. Once you've brought in an accountant and a bookkeeper, they will send you your P&L on a monthly basis. Sit with them, and make sure you understand these numbers and their significance in your business.

- **Balance Sheet.** This financial statement reports on a business's assets, which are the things you own within your business versus its liabilities, or the things that cost the business money, and how much equity you have in the business at any given time. Many practitioners are the sole owners of their practices, and this information will show them the value of their business.

- **Statement of Cash Flow.** Your statement of cash flow gives you an idea of how much cash flow you have each month. Where does your money actually sit every thirty days? This gives you an idea as to where you can start looking into spending for future months. This document starts to get a little advanced but is a good one to be aware of when speaking with your accountant or bookkeeper.

NUMBERS YOU NEED TO KNOW MONTHLY

Once you understand the basic terms and statements, it's time to look into some of the numbers you need to know on a recurring basis.

- **Profit.** This term was mentioned already, but now we look at it as a number or dollar amount, not simply as a term. What is left over each month after all of your expenses are paid? Look at your P&L, and find out what the profit line looks like. Successful businesses consistently work to grow their profit margins or at the very least, maintain their profitability. You should be monitoring this regularly.

- **Cost of Acquisition.** This number, or dollar amount, is calculated by dividing the total cost of marketing in a specific channel by the number of health consumers you gained from that investment. What does it cost to acquire a customer from each of the marketing streams you use? In the health and wellness space, this number is either at one extreme or the other. A clinic or healthcare organization knows their number down to the decimal because they use it as a resource, or they have no idea what it is. Those at the latter end of the spectrum don't invest in customer acquisition, so they rely on cost-free methods, which usually means time and energy.

- **Lifetime Value of a Client or Patient.** This is the measurement of a patient/client's long-term financial contribution to your business. This is an important number to know because it justifies how much time or money you spend on marketing or acquiring them as a patient. On average, when people come into your business, how often are they actively investing in their care? What are they paying, on average, to work with you? There are different metrics you can use here, but I like to use a three-year benchmark because most people are going to make their biggest investment with regard to their health inside of a thirty-six-month window.

- ▶ **New Leads.** This is the number of new people you're bringing onto your mailing list each month. At first, this number can be a combined number of new leads from all marketing sources, but you should get granular as you grow. Eventually, you can get to a place where new leads can be broken down by channel—leads from social media ads, leads from a website opt-in form—which will allow you to target the areas that are working well.

- ▶ **Conversions to Patients.** How many leads are converted into patients? Were the new leads qualified, meaning were they patients who fit into your niche? Does your message resonate with them? If so, it's usually simpler to convert them into patients. You should know how many people converted and the ratio of leads to patients.

This may seem like a lot of information to gather, but you can create a system or process for capturing it in less than a day. Then, schedule a few hours each month to update and track these numbers. As your team grows, you will be able to onboard people who can take these tasks off your plate, opening up more of your time for more strategic activities.

Run your numbers like you run your bloodwork: analyze them,

and let the numbers tell you what's going on. These numbers and concepts are so important to your business because they are an acknowledgement of your transformational process. In order to know whether or not you are truly helping people, while growing your business, you need to see if your numbers are headed in the right direction.

If you would like a template to help you track these numbers in your business, head to impactmedicinebook.com/resources.

PASSIVE INCOME CONFUSION

When it comes to money and finances, two concepts in particular require clarification, especially if you are going to scale a practice in our industry. The concepts of 'passive income' and 'diversified income' are used interchangeably, but they are not the same. Let me explain.

Passive income is money that you earn regularly, maybe daily or monthly, with very little effort. It's like owning a piece of real estate and renting out the property. Sure, you need to monitor the space and make occasional repairs, but you don't need to be in the kitchen making breakfast. Owning a bed and breakfast in addition to your practice is diversified income. Letting someone else run the B&B from the property that you own, that is passive income. Usually, you need to diversify before you can reap the benefits of the passive part.

For a clinician entrepreneur, the first step towards diversifying your income is to create a source of diversified revenue. In our industry, diversified revenue can come in the form of an online programme, group care or paid speaking opportunities. Over time, and when these opportunities can be scaled and leveraged without your ongoing presence, they can become a source of more passive income. This concept is critical to understand because the management of your time and the choices you make to get there are predicated on a sound understanding of the concept.

NUMBERS WON'T LIE

There's a lot of emotion around opening a business, and how your closest allies react will often come down to their own relationship with risk. For some, when they see your excitement, they will tell you everything you want to hear. Others, especially the most risk-averse of the crew, will have a hard time hiding their apprehension at your not finding a 'real job'. Family and friends, especially, will cater to your emotions.

Numbers, however, won't lie. If you've come up with a marketing strategy that's inefficient, your numbers will let you know. If something isn't set up properly, your numbers will highlight the missing points. That's the best part about having a system of statements and numbers that you can view at any time. This is also the thing that we fear the most. But we shouldn't. Our offering has the capacity to change the world. Never has there been more chronic disease to manage than right now. We are needed and desired more than ever. With a sound strategy in place, your numbers will leave you with nothing to fear.

Other key advice for properly managing your finances include the following:

- **Get a bank account for your business.** You don't want to mix your personal and business bank accounts. Separate the two.
- **Get a credit card for your business.** Again, don't use your personal one. You might need to build up some credit for your business first, but as soon as you can get a credit card for it, get one. (Advanced maneuver: Get a credit card that provides you with travel points or a related benefit. There is nothing like enjoying after-tax benefits through points on your credit card.)
- **Manage the record-keeping of your accounting in software.** You need a proper piece of software to manage your business—a manual process won't suffice.
- **Hire a bookkeeper.** Hire an expert to manage those numbers for you.
- **File your taxes.** Do this every single year. Own your finances the way you own your health.
- **Know how much it costs to operate your business each month.** Whether you are working in someone else's clinic or your own, you need to operate as a business. Know your costs.
- **Know how much you want to earn personally each month and year.** What is your target goal? What do you want to earn, and what does your business need to generate in order for you to reach this goal?
- **Track your key financial performance metrics each month.** This is basically business adulting. It's

like handing a patient a list that tells them to drink water and get equivalent rest every night. They are the fundamentals.

THE SIMPLEST FORM OF MATH

You don't need a PhD in finance to put these practices into place. This is simple math. If you can add, subtract and multiply, you can do this. Even if you can't, there's always a calculator. When the numbers get bigger and more complicated, you will be far enough along to hire people who do have finance degrees and who enjoy putting numbers together.

If you don't like math, I get it. I remember being in high school, learning about calculus and some random equations placed under a triangle. The teacher was rambling on, and all I could think about was how I was going to use this later in life. I raised my hand and asked the teacher that exact question.

'Meghan', she said. 'There isn't a single astronaut who could calculate the trajectory into space without this math'. My jaw hit the floor. There was 0 per cent chance that I was going to become an astronaut. This, however, is not that kind of math.

When good people make good money, they can do good things. I'm talking about you now, a good person who can do even more good things when they have the financial backing to do so—the financial backing that's possible with your education, with your practice and by knowing your numbers.

CHECK-IN

1. What is holding me back from hiring a bookkeeper?
2. Do I know how to access a basic summary of my important financial numbers each month?
3. Can I set some time aside now to collect and review my numbers each month?

CHAPTER 20

SETTING YOUR FEES

When I was a teenager, I was home one day watching TV, and I watched an infomercial about poverty-stricken kids in war-torn countries. The visuals showed kids in horrific conditions, and I felt so badly for them. I wanted to help in any way I could, so I did the only thing I could think of: I went to the drawer where I knew my mom kept her emergency credit card, called into the hotline and donated enough money to sponsor several children.

She can't get mad at me, I told myself as I did it. Of course, she was mad. But that memory still sticks with me. It was the beginning of a philanthropic journey that continues today.

I brought up this topic during a speaking engagement a few years ago. I was in front of a group of practitioners—roughly 80 per cent of them women from the ages of twenty-eight to fifty. They were either in the beginning of their career or in their prime and not yet thinking about retirement or life after practicing. When I asked them this question, they looked at me like I was in the wrong room: 'What kind of philanthropists do you want to be next year'?

Finally, one person spoke up. 'What do you mean by philanthropy? Because to me, a philanthropist is an old wealthy man with a trust fund or two'.

The talk went on, and I continued to get very little visual feedback from my audience. The place was quiet, and I started to get nervous. I couldn't read the room. Was I that far off-base, raising the topic of philanthropy to this crowd? Afterward, I went to the bathroom and was surprised to find several attendees crying. It hadn't occurred to them that they had a chance to impact lives through philanthropy or gain control over their finances, at least not this early in their careers. They were moved and overwhelmed at the possibility of responsibility at that level.

Over the course of the event, these women became aware of an ability they didn't know they had. They were given the tools to create a level of financial autonomy that would allow them to start giving back right away. Not only could they generate an income equal to their worth, but they could also do great things with their wealth. This was not a zero-sum game. This was more a matter of having their cake and eating it too.

What kind of philanthropist do you want to be? And what has to happen to allow you to be that type of philanthropist right now?

SETTING THE FEES YOU DESERVE

The time-for-money trap lures in many practitioners. Nearly everyone is doing it this way. The transactional model lends itself to avoiding financial innovation and encourages pricing that likens your offer to everyone else's within a geographical area.

Getting out of this trap is necessary if you want to create a financial life untethered to your time. While diversifying your offers into the Quadrants of Care will provide more leverage, ending the time-for-money model can be as simple as acknowledging that it is not your time that people are seeking; it is your *strategy*.

Remember that in addition to being a practitioner, you are an entrepreneur. And entrepreneurs get paid to deliver results and outcomes, and the pricing structure needs to account for the risk you take on as the owner.

Depending on your location of practice and the restrictions on your licence, you will not necessarily have access to all of these models. Let's look at some options:

▶ **Insurance.** This is a great model for patients but rarely compensates allied health practitioners effectively for their work. Insurance companies are caught in a time-for-money paradigm that incentivizes volume and eventually, burnout. This model comes at a cost to practitioners, and I don't advocate for it. Innovate your offering to reach more people.

▶ **Memberships.** This model works well for primary care practices. It enables practitioners to recoup some of the administrative costs surrounding continuity of care, and it guarantees recurring revenue. This model does not lend itself well to high-ticket offerings as it becomes confusing for your customers to understand what you are actually delivering.

- **Packages.** This is by-far my favourite option. If you are permitted to charge in 'block fees', it is my recommendation that you create financial packages that correspond to your transformational programme. The more people pay up front, the less risk there is to you. You can pass this savings on to your patients. Generally, paying in full results in a 10 per cent discount over a monthly payment plan or a three-payment option.
- **Fee for Service.** Ugh. If you are forced to charge patients at each visit due to your regulation, then this is likely your best option. It is also the highest-risk model for compensation. There is no financial incentive for retention, and most practitioners don't charge enough in their first few visits to account for the time they spend on the case once the patient leaves their office. Furthermore, it puts you in a situation where you are constantly 'selling' the patient as to why they need to keep spending. Even if you explain that this is simply the pricing logistics associated with transformation, it feels like the patient is getting nickeled and dimed.
- **Hybrid Package/Fee for Service.** This is the next best option to packages, and it is 'allowed' in any jurisdiction. If I went back to seeing patients, this is how I would design my fee schedule. Deploying this model requires that you transition your appointments from 'blocks of

time' to 'types of strategy'. This model requires that you charge more at the beginning of your relationship with a patient, when you are spending the most amount of time on their case. This means that you will increase the pricing on your Discovery Phase and early appointments in the Active Phase of Care. Once you get through the first four to five visits, the price can drop to reflect your familiarization with their case and decrease in time you spend after appointments. By openly lowering your fees past visit four to five, you are additionally incentivizing the patient to 'stick with it' to access a preferable rate. This model drives retention and lowers your financial risk. Win-win.

Let's look at how this would compare to a Fee for Service model.

Fee for Service Model for Average Rates:
- Intake Appointment: $250
- Follow-Up Appointments: $125
- Total Revenue after Intake Plus Five Follow-Ups: $875

Hybrid Model with Progressive Rates:
- Discover Phase: Two appointments.
  - Intake: $475
  - Disclosure appointment: $225
- Active Phase of Care Starter Appointments (until visit 4): $175

- ▸ Active Phase of Care Momentum Appointments (post visit 4): $158
- ▸ Total Revenue after Discovery Phase Plus Five Follow-Ups: $1,558

More detail and training on all of these options can be found at impactmedicinebook.com/resources

> You help more people by innovating your offer,
> not lowering your prices.

NEGOTIATING YOUR FEES

There has been much discussion around fee structures and what to charge patients, but what about what *you* are being charged to operate out of an office? For anyone working inside of a clinic and working on a split—a 60/40 profit split, for example—fees must be approved by the clinic owner. And if you are a junior associate with only a fraction of the experience compared to other practitioners inside the clinic, it could be hard to negotiate the rates you want to charge.

Do your research ahead to time to see if you are a good fit for the clinic. Is this going to lead you to the freedom you need and to working with the target patient you're looking to treat? Know which kind of clinic you are going to work in beforehand. And consider laying the financial upside on the table for the clinic owner. Ensure that you are working in an environment that is equally committed to your growth and theirs. Remember, sometimes you are not in the right place. If you are committed to running a progressive business and your clinic owner is not, it might be time for you to go.

Remember that your financial autonomy is directly correlated to your capacity to impact your practice, your family and your community. It is not correlated with your financial struggle. Reaching more people through innovative offerings like those discussed in these chapters is what moves the needle.

FINAL THOUGHTS ON MONEY

Necessity brings capacity. When you really need to know these skills, you will increase your ability to learn them. Earlier in this chapter, I talked about a speech I gave around philanthropy to a group of colleagues. During that same event, I was told, 'Meghan, this is all great stuff, but I don't want to wait ten years to grow my business'.

It doesn't have to take ten years. It can happen right now, but you need to *want* it to happen now. If you want to attract wealth and stability in your life, you need to focus on it. When I was asked how to make the growth happen sooner, I was not in a hall or private corner; I was asked the question while on stage. I thought for a moment and then threw the question back to the audience member. 'Does your partner like their job'? I asked. She shook her head. 'Then why not invite them to retire early. Let them know you will handle it from here'. She sat there, stunned.

The thing is, if you don't really need the money, there will always be something that gets in the way of the strategic action, the increase in fees or the difficult conversation. Focus on what you want and take the informed and strategic risks to make it happen. Get some skin in the game, and attract what you really want into your life.

That's the sort of jolt, the *vision*, you sometimes need to get things moving in the right direction. You have to be hungry. Think about why you took on all this debt to pursue this profession in the first place. Why did you take on all that financial risk? Why did you invest so much of your time? What prompted you to become a practitioner? What matters to you in all of this?

This is how thinking like an entrepreneur comes into play. Entrepreneurship is messy. It's hard. Very few things will be simple, and if this idea of transforming healthcare for your patients doesn't really matter to you, then you will be in for a bumpy ride.

CHECK-IN

1. Do my fees and pricing model need to be adjusted to account for my strategy and risk as a business owner?
2. If I deployed a hybrid model next month, what would be the increase in revenue?
3. What mindset or fixed beliefs about money emerged as I read through this section?

PART FIVE:
CENTS AND SENSE—KEY TAKEAWAYS

The thinking that goes into the financial modelling of healthcare delivery on the practitioner side of the equation is alarmingly unsophisticated. This significantly destabilizes the industry because of the lack of financial stability and growth for the providers—but it does not have to be that way.

You now have a framework for thinking about money, seeing the numbers in your business and knowing what they mean, then thinking about your own fee structure and whether it needs to change.

By not acknowledging the true cost of care, we are perpetuating a system of elite medicine that is accessible only to those who can afford to work without adequate compensation.

An entrepreneur has the capacity to deliver tremendous impact while simultaneously having the privilege of earning a living from what they do in the world. This is not a zero-sum game. You can have your cake and eat it too. The entrepreneur understands that the financial piece becomes a vehicle that drives their impact faster. This is what it means to think like an entrepreneur.

For more IMPACT Medicine resources, visit
impactmedicinebook.com/resources.

PART SIX

THINKING LIKE AN ENTREPRENEUR

'If opportunity doesn't knock, build a door'.

—Milton Berle

Entrepreneurship: *are we born this way, or do we learn to become entrepreneurs?*

This is a question I have asked entrepreneurs to comment upon in over three hundred episodes of my podcast. There is still no consensus. Some openly admit that they were born an entrepreneur, while others note that it was the only recourse for their passion. As for me, I know that this was my natural inclination. Having been fired from the only real job I have held, I would certify that I am 100 per cent unemployable. With that said, having had the opportunity to work with thousands of entrepreneurs in my practice, podcast and businesses, I know that effective entrepreneur -ing is also a set of skills that you can learn.

If you have gotten this far into IMPACT Medicine, no doubt you have some inclination towards both the genetic and mission-driven motivation that informs entrepreneurship. Refining this inclination takes practice, curiosity, a tenacious approach to failure and the courage to risk rejection. All of these skills and attitudes are refined with practice and exposure, so buckle up.

The exciting part of being an entrepreneur is that you get to write your own rules and set the stage for your own story. There will be challenges, but there will be challenges in life either way. In an era where chronic disease remains one of the single largest threats towards humanity, you need to step into your element as a clinician entrepreneur.

Some practitioners have a timid start. They want a taste of what entrepreneurship offers. I'm more of a 'cake and eat it too' kind of entrepreneur. I believe that if I'm going to work this hard and accept the risk that comes with doing it my way, I want (and expect/attract) it all. I want the money and the time, and I want to make an impact. I want a high-quality life that exceeds my grandest expectations. I want this for you too.

This section represents the insights and patterns of thinking that I bring to my businesses and the businesses of those I consult. It is the thinking that has enabled me to build multiple companies that impact lives, including those of my family, beyond my wildest dreams.

Everything you create begins with how you think and the quality of thoughts and actions you produce.

Tony Robbins, my best-friend-in-my-own-mind since I started listening to him on tapes in high school, has said that the quality of your life is tied to the quality of your questions. I really believe that too. So, I have two questions for you—questions that will inspire you, right in this very moment, to begin thinking like an entrepreneur:

1. *How can I solve* _____ *problems better and less expensively than the next best option?*

   For example, if you know how to help women manage premenstrual headaches, you know that your competition is Advil. So, how do you solve premenstrual headaches better than Advil? How do you define the problem better and provide better value? If you can't provide the solution at a lower cost, you must somehow provide and articulate a superior solution.

2. *How can* _____ *opportunity lower my costs, increase my revenue or expedite my version of impact?*

As an entrepreneur, your ventures and actions must satisfy one of these three objectives. Without this focus, you risk chasing endless 'big, shiny objects'. They look great, but they are distractions that won't get you what you want or lead you to where you want to go. (And if you don't know where you are going, head back to Part One: Intention.) Keep this question in mind. Make it your mantra. Avoid the 'big, shiny object' syndrome.

Now, let's delve deeper into the levers that will heighten your effectiveness as a clinician entrepreneur.

CHAPTER 21

BRINGING YOUR IMPACT TO LIFE

E ntrepreneurship can accelerate the transformation and growth of almost every area of your life. As an entrepreneur, you have the privilege of uncapped potential in what you do, how much you make and the impact you have on the world.

The intersection of health-mastery, mindset and entrepreneurship is a science I call Entrepology. In studying this science and working towards the endless expansion of each of these elements, I designed a system to check in on the specific areas of growth that can accompany life as an entrepreneur. I call this the Entrepology Life System (ELS), and we explored these concepts in Part One: Intention. The ELS is comprised of eight concepts that empower the Entrepologist (someone committed to expanding their health, mindset and entrepreneurial impact) and propels them towards the highest levels of transformation, growth and impact.

THE ENTREPOLOGY LIFE SYSTEM

Like most parents, I want to make a contribution to this world that outlives me, and I want my children to see that contribution, knowing that it is within their power to make major contributions to the world as well. This system provides a series of checks and balances on your growth, blind spots and strengths.

Think of the eight concepts as points on a pinwheel, with your ideal life at the centre. When all the points are spinning in harmony, your best life is humming. It's all possible with this system.

THE ENTREPOLOGY LIFE SYSTEM

Figure 12: The Entrepology Life System describes the core areas of potential growth and self-actualization expedited through the entrepreneurial journey.

ELS Concept #1: Purpose

Being an Entrepologist—or any type of entrepreneur—grants you the opportunity to align your work with your life's purpose.

As an Entrepologist, you are able to offer access to upstream healing systems of medicine to many more people. This is my vision and my purpose, and it fuels my passion for the work. Being paid to pursue this vision and fulfil my purpose is an added bonus.

ELS Concept #2: Impact

Entrepreneurship enables you to have an impact you desire to create. (Highlight that.) Regardless of the type of business you run, running a company or practice enables you to impact the people who work for you, your colleagues and your clients. You have the power to set a culture you believe in and invite others to enjoy that culture with you. You can empower other women, promote diversity and show people a better way to work.

You get to define the impact you want to make and the metrics that inform your progress. Unlike purpose, IMPACT refers to the breadth and strength of your actions. Start by defining who and in what way you want to impact people's lives. Next, add the metrics that will inform whether you are on track.

ELS Concept #3: Complete Control of Your Income and Finances

One of the easiest ways to crush someone's motivation to make an impact is to cap their income. People in traditional jobs where their salary is controlled and limited by their employer are incentivized differently to innovate and grow. Can you blame them? After all, compared with the unlimited payoff available to the entrepreneur, a practitioner in a traditional working situation has much less to gain by taking risks personally and financially. It is a different game entirely.

Taking control of your income is especially important for women because we are at a disadvantage when it comes to money. We are statistically paid less than men for doing the same work. Women receive less investment capital, are approved for smaller loans and are frequently socialized not to have to speak about money. This ends *today*. As an entrepreneur, regardless of gender, you and only you must decide to take control of your financial destiny. When you have the money and understand how to leverage it to your advantage, you will experience a new version of autonomy. You can do great things with your money but only if you have the knowledge to manage it effectively.

ELS Concept #4: Spiritual, Intellectual and Emotional Growth

Entrepreneurship, and the drive to fulfil your life's mission, will affect internal growth for you spiritually, intellectually and emotionally. There is no way around it. You will have to make decisions about your career and your business without relying on others to make them for you. You will face challenges, meet people and acquire skills that enable the expansion of each of these areas of your life.

ELS Concept #5: Autonomy over Relationships in Your Life

Many of my closest friends are entrepreneurs. Why? Because we are all growing on the same trajectory. We understand each other's challenges. They are not questioning why I would want to earn or impact more. They are driven by the same motivating factors. These are the kinds of people I like to be around. We all contribute to each other's growth, and we cheer on each other's success. And yet, while I have been blessed to grow around other entrepreneurs, I am equally committed to my other circles of family and friends. ELS concept #5 is an equal call to action to ensure that our dedication to work does not overshadow the time and presence we want to hold for everyone in our life.

ELS Concept #6: Experiential Living

What experiences do you want to have in your life? Do you want to work for ten years, so you can afford to take your family on a trip to Disneyland? Are you envisioning the trip of a lifetime when you retire? I don't want to wait until I'm seventy years old to enjoy the fruits of my labour. Life for all of us started many years ago, and if you haven't begun really living it, you can decide to start living—really living—right now.

Entrepreneurism makes that possible. You can run your own business and travel. You can write that book you always wanted to write. You can go where you want to go and do what you want to do with no one and no one job standing in your way.

You can have your cake and eat it too. You can even combine your career and experiential living. If there is a place you want to visit, there is probably a conference, a client, or a speaking opportunity that can get you there. Stack your desires.

ELS Concept #7: Health

I spent most of my clinical career working with entrepreneurs, including clinicians, trying to restore their health. Don't give up your health to build the business of your dreams. Strategy and its accompanying decisions will move you further from burnout. This entire book is a roadmap away from overworking.

ELS Concept #8: Legacy

Legacy comes in several forms: intellectual, philanthropic and through health and genetics. Leveraging the ACTION Framework and creating a transformational system is your opportunity to create a legacy around your unique approach and the intellectual capital you are accumulating in practice. What type of legacy are you living and building in each of these areas?

THE JOURNEY IS AS IMPORTANT AS THE OUTCOME

Pursuing entrepreneurship is not just about working long days, building a business or hoping that someday all your hard work will pay off. The journey is as worthwhile as the payoff, and as you build your business and grow spiritually, intellectually and emotionally, you'll benefit by virtue from the person you are becoming. Your goal is to be that person who lives up to your intention and, ideally, your purpose.

The Entrepology Life System is a framework, not a rule. Check in regularly to make sure you are on track. I have included a brief check-in for you at the end of this chapter to help highlight where you may need to direct some personal attention towards yourself as CEO.

Remember, your life will forever be moving in and out of seasons. Rating these elements of the ELS is not about scoring the highest; it is about bringing awareness to the areas that may require more attention, now or later. Practice being aware without being judgemental. (Highlight that too.)

CHECK-IN

Rate, on a scale from 1 to 10, and with 10 being the highest score, score your sense of strength in each of the Entrepology Life System sections.

1. How strong is my personal sense of purpose? _____/10
2. Do I feel that I am having the impact I desire? _____/10
3. Am I currently where I want to be financially? _____/10
4. How much ongoing growth do I feel I am acquiring...
   a. Spiritually? _____/10
   b. Intellectually? _____/10
   c. Personally? _____/10
5. How well do I feel I am doing currently with my important relationships? _____/10
6. Am I having the types of life experiences I desire? _____/10
7. How well do I feel I am doing at attending to and optimizing my health? _____/10
8. How strongly do I feel that I am developing a legacy
   a. Intellectually? _____/10
   b. Financially? _____/10
   c. Through my health? _____/10

CHAPTER 22

MAKING AN IMPACT WITH YOUR TIME

T ime, not money, is our most precious resource. Yet, as practitioners, most of us don't design our schedules to maximize our time. We tend to do the opposite—chasing money while sacrificing precious time. It's not uncommon for a practitioner who's just starting out to be running from one clinic to a second, third or fourth, juggling schedules instead of using that time to make an impact.

As an entrepreneur, you have to think differently. You must value your time, and your unique skills to be deployed within your time, as your most precious assets.

Ironically, we are very good at creating more quality time for our patients. Think about it: by optimizing health and one's quality of life, we create access to higher quality time. We give them more time to live pain-free or energetic lives. Ultimately, our area of expertise allows us to create and sell quality time. When you think about it that way, you can see just how valuable our 'product'—and the time we devote to it—really is!

As clinicians, we do not honour this value system with our own time. It's not uncommon for a practitioner to devote 60 per cent of their work time to seeing patients. They get paid for this time. But the work doesn't stop there because they then have to spend time with charting, following up and working with staff, which eats up another 30 per cent, unpaid.

These percentages do not allow time for growth or work *on* a business. Working more hours isn't the answer. Instead, practitioners must find ways to decrease the time they spend on other activities, so they can devote that time to business growth.

Networking, building relationships and finding opportunities for reciprocity pay off in the long run, but only if you commit the time to them up front. Building a business is a long game. You are playing the game either way, and the sooner you decide to make choices that align with your desired future, the faster you will get there.

Changing how you spend your time as the CEO of your company is the single most important factor in determining your long-term stability. It is the inflexion point where practitioners go from treading water to learning how to swim. It is literally how you start to get ahead.

THE DIRECTION OF ANY BUSINESS CAN BE PREDICTED BASED ON HOW ITS LEADER SPENDS THEIR TIME

60%

Time available to
see patients

30%

Admin,
Research, F/U

5%

Business
Building

5%

Strategy &
Relationships

ALLOCATION OF A STRATEGIC CLINICIAN C.E.O.

25%

Time available to
see patients

15%

Admin,
Research, F/U

30%

Business
Building

30%

Strategy &
Relationships

Figures 13a and 13b: These two figures describe the time allocation of clinician entrepreneurs before and after they begin to diversify their income and allocate their time to reflect their role as a strategist in their business. You will not have the time or capacity to diversify your business if you are seeing patients more than 30 per cent of your working week. The movement from 60 per cent to 25 per cent is a process that happens over time as your new income streams adequately support your income.

DIVIDING TIME: THE FIVE CATEGORIES

I've attended conferences and read books and blogs about structuring time to be more efficient and boost productivity. Most of them included some valuable takeaways, but none of them fit the way I work and live. I prefer more freedom and flexibility with my time, so I developed my own structure. When I thought about how I utilize time, I came up with five main categories. This works for me, and it may work for you too, but consider it a framework that you can tweak to suit your lifestyle. The most important element for you to recognize is that not all time is created equally.

Deep Dive Days

On my Deep Dive Days, I block the entire day and dedicate that time to move a project forward. Think, *Head down, no distractions.* No calls, no texts, no meetings and no exceptions. Deep Dive Days are highly productive, but only if I stick to my own rules around them: no reading emails and no lunch plans with friends or family. I begin the day with a clearly stated goal, and I'm on a mission to get it done. My family and my team know when I have a Deep Dive Day on the schedule, and they honour it by leaving me to do my work.

I try to get in at least one Deep Dive Day a week. You will be amazed at how much you can accomplish when you remove all the tasks, activities and distractions from your life to focus on making sizable progress on one project. I use Deep Dive Days for strategizing and making content.

Momentum Moments

If you can't find time in your schedule to do an entire Deep Dive Day, add Momentum Moments. These are smaller blocks on your calendar dedicated to making significant progress on a project or completing a task in a few hours. The same rules apply: no email, texts or phone calls and no interruptions. Plan to commit at least two to three hours to a Momentum Moment or half a day if you can.

Schedule Momentum Moments during times when your energy and productivity are at their highest peaks. Some people are super productive first thing in the morning, while others peak in the late morning, and still others do their best work in the evening. Block out Momentum Moments during your peak times for superior results.

Stage Days

Stage Days are the opposite of Deep Dive Days and Momentum Moments. These are your client-facing days. Skilled clinician entrepreneurs devote this time to seeing patients, and they do so efficiently. This means no working on side projects or answering email between patients. It's the 25 per cent of your work hours, for which you are being paid, so commit this time fully to patients.

Prepare for this time to make the most of it. Set an email response to let people know that you are seeing patients and won't be responding to their messages immediately. Prep your charts before the day begins. Go into your Stage Days fully prepared, and you will enjoy them more, confident that your mind and your schedule are clear and you are totally focussed on the people who are paying you for results.

Follow-Through Days

Follow-Through Days are for dealing with all of your administrative tasks. Finish your charting, catch up on emails and return phone calls. These tasks will likely not take your whole day, so add relationship-building activities into these days as well. You might be able to complete all your administrative tasks in the morning and dedicate the afternoon to networking.

You'll be tempted to squeeze in some Follow-Through Days activities on your Stage Days, but fight that urge. To fully connect with patients, you need to maintain a state of high energy and clear focus, which isn't possible when you're shifting gears and diverting your attention away from the people in front of you to attend to other tasks.

As your business grows, you can hand off some of your Follow-Through Days tasks to your team. This allows you more time for building your business.

Play Days

These days have been around forever in the corporate world—some people refer to them as golfing (because that's exactly what many executives do on their Play Days). Whether you like to golf, play tennis or even go to the movies, find something you enjoy and go out and play. This isn't family time, by the way. It's still part of your working hours. But you are getting out, meeting people, trying something new and expanding your horizons, basically. You're having new experiences, maybe learning and definitely having fun. When you have fun and step away from your work, you leave space for new ideas and creative flow to intersect your work.

YOUR IMPACT POWERS

Every practitioner knows that feeling of trying to catch up with work late in the evening, when it seems like the entire world is asleep. I was certainly no different. Around eleven o'clock one night, I was in my office finishing up a diet diary for a patient. I was exhausted. I suddenly realized the absurdity of what I was doing. What did it matter what a person ate or drank every day, if they weren't using their time in a way that energized their life? I certainly wasn't feeling energized. I was wiped out and approaching burnout. I couldn't continue spending time helping patients with their energy levels while completely ignoring my own.

That gave me an idea. I imagined my energy as a series of concentric circles. In the centre, I wrote down the types of work that made me feel the most energized. These were activities that I call my IMPACT Powers. It's the work that I love to do, and it also happens to drive growth for my business. Your IMPACT Powers may be different than mine, but make sure they contribute to your business's growth.

IMPACT POWERS REQUIRE CLARITY & HONESTY

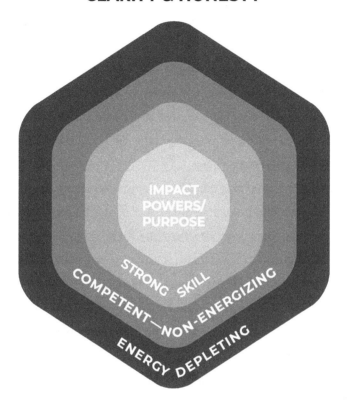

Energy depleting—You are not good at these tasks and they make you feel frustrated and out of momentum.

Competent—Non-Energizing—You are adequate at these tasks, but other people are way more talented and passionate about their completion.

Strong Skill—You have some serious skill, but you are not passionate about these skills.

Impact Powers—This is a one-of-a kind skill.

Figure 14: IMPACT Powers are the skills you uniquely bring to your business. They are part of what will drive your brand and success.

Around the circle of IMPACT Powers is the first ring, which comprises your High-Energy Strong Skills. This is the work that you're passionate about, but it doesn't necessarily drive business growth.

The next ring includes tasks in which you are competent, but these tasks don't energize you. These could be things like scheduling your social media posts—they may be simple to do, but they aren't aligned with your impact energy. We'll call those Medium Energy Competencies.

Finally, the outer ring consists of Energy-Depleting Necessities. This is the work that zaps your energy, but it must be done. For some practitioners, there is nothing they (me) dread more than charting.

When you are at a point in your business where you can delegate tasks, look first to this outer ring. Hiring a medical scribe for your charting means no more hours expending your own energy on that task. Work from the outside in, but don't give up your IMPACT Powers. Hang on to that work for yourself.

Spending more time in your IMPACT Powers state of mind will not only energize you, but it will also make you happier. You'll be doing the work you love, and when it's all finished, you won't feel depleted. That energy will continue to power you through the rest of your day, whatever you choose to do with that time.

VALUE YOUR TIME

We're all different in so many ways. We may have different genders, races and appearances. We come from a variety of socioeconomic worlds and global geographies. As different as we are, all humans share a common limiting denominator: our time. No matter who we are in the world, each of us gets only so much time. What we do with that time is up to the individual.

Scheduling my time to capitalize on my IMPACT Powers and the five categories of time has allowed me to accomplish more of what matters and take back more of my time. I update my calendar regularly and share it with my team every week; they know when I'm available and when I'm out of touch. They know my Deep Dive Days and my Stage Days, and they don't expect a speedy response to their emails on those days. They know my Play Days too, and they don't try to engage me on those days. They respect my time because I respect my time. I respect their time too, and I maintain that transparency in my schedule, so they aren't left waiting around for me to return their calls and emails.

That last part is important because your time isn't more valuable than anybody else's. Disrespecting your team's, your colleagues' and your patients' time is unprofessional. Making people wait for long periods of time in an exam room sends the message that your time is more valuable than theirs. This is not the case, and it's not the message you want to send to those people whose health is in your hands.

Value your time, protect it and move away from this idea of trading time for money. Until you master your use of time, it will be impossible for you to move forward in your business. Which is what we unpack next, the Ascension journey.

CHECK-IN

1. What per cent of my working week do I currently spend seeing patients one-to-one?

2. What tasks am I completing each week that *could* be done by someone else?

3. Block your schedule by colour for the next quarter. Each colour block should correspond to a type of time. For resources on bringing your schedule to life in this way, visit impactmedicinebook.com/resources

CHAPTER 23

THE FIVE STAGES OF ASCENSION

N aturopathic Doctors (and I am sure, other allied practitioners) fresh out of school have traditionally been presented with three tracks when launching their careers. These were the options presented to me when I first began practicing. At the time, I failed to recognize how limiting they were to my career and my life.

The first option was to join someone else's practice as an associate or start my own. In this model, I would see patients all day and have evenings and weekends off—the typical nine-to-five (or seven-to-seven, six-to-eight, or longer) workday. My income would be dictated by the hours I spent with patients and capped by the amount of time I spent in one-to-one interactions with them.

The second option was to work as a sales representative for a supplier while also seeing patients. I could see patients for designated hours each week and use the rest of my available time to sell medical devices or equipment to hospitals or clinics. This would allow me to make more money and sever the tie between hours worked and incomes earned, but I didn't relish the idea of selling products when I'd rather be working with patients.

The third option was to work for the government, evaluating and approving natural health products. This was a sought-after position due to the low risk involved. Some practitioners liked the idea of working within the government, even though they understood they were still limiting their incomes to whatever the job paid.

None of these options offered promises of Ascension. The safety they offered came with a greater risk—the risk of accepting a role in which I was destined to stagnate.

Most people who decided to study health sciences did so because we wanted to be helpers. Yet, we were given options that lacked vision for how we could leverage our hard-earned, expensive degrees and our deep desires to reach more people with our expertise. Limited to these options and at a loss for better ideas, many practitioners made their choice and settled for a career and a life that never quite lived up to their aspirations.

THREE NEW PHASES OF A PRACTITIONER'S CAREER

Today, practitioners don't have to settle. The clinician entrepreneur who chooses to open her own practice has a clear path—three distinct phases followed by five stages of Ascension. No tying your income to your time. No income cap. And no doing work that you never wanted to do in the first place.

Phase 1: Launch and Learn

The first of these phases is called the Launch and Learn phase. Everyone starts here. I refer to this as the 'sink or swim' phase. Picture the excited new grad jumping off a boat and into the clear blue ocean of career possibility. Moments—or six to eighteen months—later, that same grad is tired, waterlogged and struggling to stay afloat. No one mentioned it would be this hard. If their head is still above water, it is often struggling to gain momentum in any particular direction.

Safety from the lack of predictability of the ocean is found on the beach, but to get there, you first need to learn how to swim.

Phase 2: Know and Grow

Launch and Learn has you jumping into the ocean and hoping for the best. In the Know and Grow phase, you're swimming with direction in mind. During this phase, the practitioner is starting to enjoy some momentum. She has a good number of consistent patients, and her one-to-one operations are running smoothly. At this point, the clinician entrepreneur must take a step back from devoting all her time working *in* the business to focus her attention on working *on* the business.

In this phase, I recommend initiating what I call the 'CEO System'. This is an intentional step you must take, or you'll wind up stuck in option #1 above, where your career is solely one-to-one care and your income potential has the same one-to-one relationship with your time. That's how you end up exhausted on the beach. When you have passed the Launch and Learn phase and are into the

Know and Grow phase, make the conscious effort to stop reacting to everyone else's 'emergencies', and commit time to the business of your practice, beginning with the CEOs: Care, Empowerment and Operational.

C is for Care strategy. Leveraging the Quadrants of Care and focussing in particular on the Strategy Quadrant, your care strategy is the unique methodology that sets your skills apart and defines your transformational process.

E is for Education-based marketing system. You need to track and organize the metrics that let you know whether you're growing or shrinking. Try different marketing strategies, test them against each other and analyse the results. Invest in those that best grow your business. Want to know more? Return to Part Four: Attraction.

O is for Operational strategy. Operations is all about the inner workings of your business and how they affect results. Think time management, money management and project and people management. Do you have standard operating procedures (SOPs), and are they documented? Are you still doing work that you could be paying someone else to do—someone who could probably do it better and charge you less than what your own time is worth? Operational strategy is a big subject that needs revisiting often, but it can make or break your business.

Phase 3: Road to IMPACT

In this third phase of your career, you are laser-focussed on delivering intentional, transformational care and adding the security of diversified income. You are now on the beach.

No more sinking or swimming. Here on the beach, you have options. You have flexibility. You don't have to stick to the traditional path of trading time for income. In keeping with the beach theme, the world is your oyster. You're on your way—on the Road to IMPACT.

You are not locked into a dead-end career with a capped income and a limited degree of impact. You have entered the first stage of Ascension, and there is only one way to go: up.

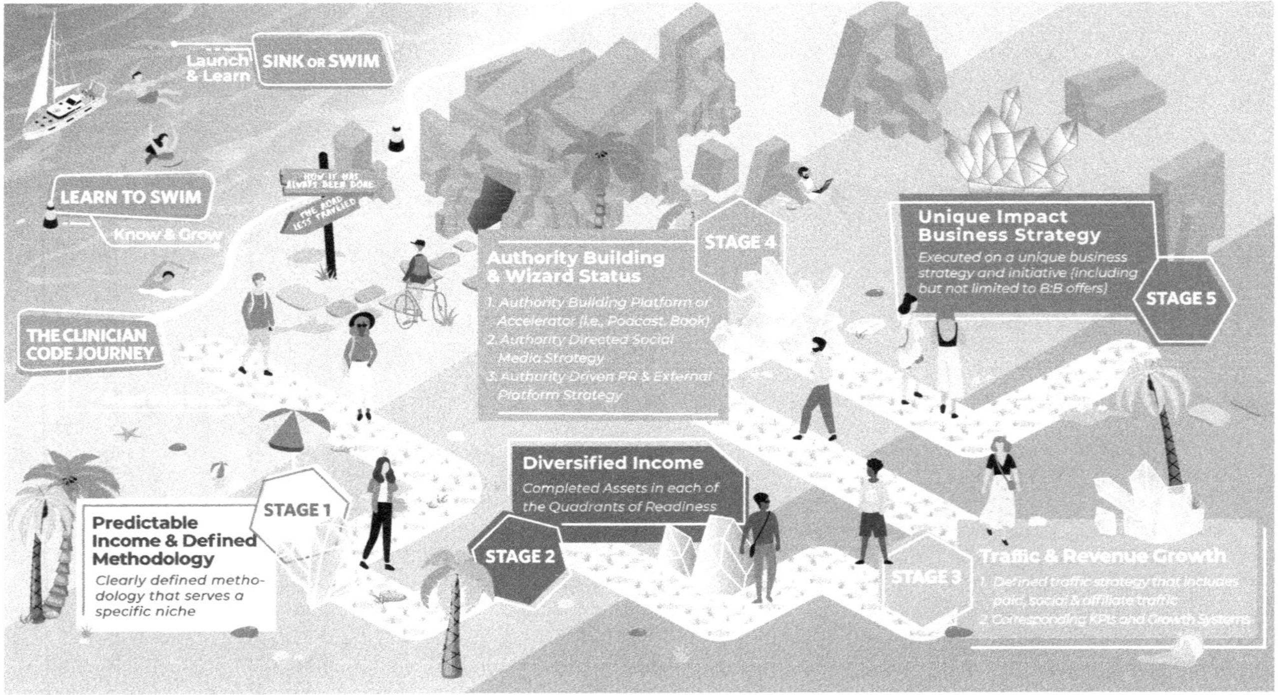
Launch & Learn
SINK OR SWIM
LEARN TO SWIM
Know & Grow
HOW IT HAS ALWAYS BEEN DONE
THE ROAD LESS TRAVELED
THE CLINICIAN CODE JOURNEY
Authority Building & Wizard Status
1. Authority Building Platform or Accelerator (i.e., Podcast, Book)
2. Authority Directed Social Media Strategy
3. Authority Driven PR & External Platform Strategy
STAGE 4
Unique Impact Business Strategy
Executed on a unique business strategy and initiative (including but not limited to B:B offers)
STAGE 5
Diversified Income
Completed Assets in each of the Quadrants of Readiness
STAGE 2
STAGE 1
Predictable Income & Defined Methodology
Clearly defined methodology that serves a specific niche
STAGE 3
Traffic & Revenue Growth
1. Defined traffic strategy that includes paid, social & affiliate traffic
2. Corresponding KPIs and Growth Systems

Figure 15: The is the code map to career Ascension. It is a bird's-eye view of what is possible beyond one-to-one, transactional care.

THE FIVE STAGES OF ASCENSION ON THE ROAD TO IMPACT

This Road to IMPACT comprises five stages, with each stage providing more momentum to move you on and up in your clinician entrepreneur journey.

Stage #1: Predictable Income and Defined Methodology

In the first stage, you need predictable income. The primary goal here is financial. You must know how much money you have coming in—and going out—every month. You may not have as much as you'd like yet, but you know what the outcome is, and you have a baseline from which to start. You can forecast with a degree of certainty how much you'll have this month, next month and the month after that. Knowing this is imperative for gaining momentum anywhere else.

The other goal in this stage is to create a defined methodology. Create your own unique transformational process, develop your own IP and give these assets a name. If you're working with an associate, create your own individual assets that are yours to take with it if you strike out on your own.

Stage #2: Diversified Income

The second stage on the Road to IMPACT entails diversifying your income. Do you want a million-dollar business? You can have it. *Anyone* can have it. You just need to be strategic about it. Once you have a defined methodology, you have an immediate opportunity to start diversifying your income. Refer to the Quadrants of Care for more direction on the opportunities to diversify your income.

Stage #3: Traffic and Revenue Growth

Diversifying your income won't deliver overnight impact or wealth. It is a starting point and an anchor for driving impact and limitless income. Here, you create growth in your business not by doing more work or creating more assets, but by selling more of what you've already created. Use your education-based marketing strategy here to create more traffic and continue to grow those revenue streams that are producing for your practice.

At the same time, you might have to tweak, or even eliminate, products and services that are underperforming. Give your health consumers more of what they want and don't confuse them with products they don't care about. Zero in on your niche market, and let them show you what they really want from you.

Stage #4: Authority Building and Wizard Status

As you move through the stages on the Road to IMPACT, you will start to distinguish yourself from other businesses. If you've started on this road with associates, you may find yourself on diverging paths. That's fine—in fact, it's totally normal. You can each build your own authority around the people and the solutions where you're finding the greatest success and that you enjoy most.

Here, you will begin to identify more opportunities for new revenue streams. You are also refining your website and building on your authority and your brand with assets such as a podcast, a book and social media channels with followers. As an authority on your defined methodology and your market, you are continuously making an impact.

Stage #5: Unique IMPACT Business Strategy

In the final stage, you can start to train others in your industry. You may be invited to be a keynote speaker at an industry event. You may find yourself being invited as a guest on other people's podcasts, and you may be interviewed by publications. You might lead a mastermind group, or you could be among other thought leaders in the industry who work together to strategize new directions in healthcare. In this stage, you have a unique vantage point in your industry because you will understand it so thoroughly that you will be able to see answers to problems that other people might not see.

You can begin to repackage and sell your assets to others in the industry at this stage, where they can then incorporate them into their own defined methodology that includes your brand.

■   ■   ■

This road doesn't only deliver greater impact and more income; it provides more security and offers more flexibility. It makes you the master of your career and your life. Now you have your own beach and your own island, and you can do whatever you want. When you get to this stage on the Road to IMPACT, celebrate. Throw yourself a beach party. Do something to recognize how far you've come, and bask in the limitless possibilities that lie ahead.

CHECK-IN

1. Which of the three phases of practice development do I think I am in currently?
2. What immediate action do I think I can take to move myself forward immediately?
3. Where do I feel that I need additional knowledge to move myself and my business forward?

CHAPTER 24

THE END IS YOUR BEGINNING

'The journey of a thousand miles begins with a single step'.

—Chinese proverb

That proverb reminds me of a story about a man who was traversing Antarctica, following a path on which others had died before him. People thought he was crazy for doing what he did, and when they asked how he was able to survive, he responded by saying, 'I just put one foot in front of the other, and I did it over and over again'.

We, as humans, tend to overcomplicate things. We vastly *over*estimate other peoples' skills while *under*estimating our own. We tend to make excuses when it comes to taking that leap of faith to improve ourselves because we feel as though we won't be able to accomplish what someone else would accomplish under similar circumstances. We bet on others better than we bet on ourselves.

Instead of paving our own paths, we take those that have already been paved. Our entire life can become a game of paint by numbers. Whether it's our formal schooling, training or anything else in life, we are told that there are certain, predetermined paths for us to take.

The clinician entrepreneur path, the Entrepology path, is like a blank canvas. You *get* to create new things and try them out. If people don't like them? That's fine. Lesson learned. Move on to the next blank canvas, and try again.

Your life is not a paint-by-numbers book. It is a framework, but there are no hard lines to stay within and no preselected colours to choose. You can make up your own colours and paint your canvas in broad strokes or fine lines. Use this book, and my own lessons, as a guide. My own Road to IMPACT included a lot of missteps because I lacked a framework to follow and build upon. My canvas wasn't exactly a work of art, at least not at first. But as I figured out what worked and what didn't, I began to create a masterpiece I was willing to hang in my living room—which is perfect because it is just for me. Use what I've learned to choose your own colours and brushes to design a version of your life that will light up *your* room.

The best clinicians I know are not the ones who follow someone else's algorithm. The best clinicians are those who can look at the whole system—what people need and what they, the clinician, have to offer—and bridge that gap with intentional choices that deliver desired outcomes for themselves and their curated market of health consumers.

When it comes to your business, you need to be anchored to where you want to go. You need to know what you want. If you're staring at that blank canvas and you have no idea what you want, nobody can help direct you. You need to start thinking about what it is that you truly want. When you give yourself full authority, you will become a better entrepreneur and clinician.

And it doesn't matter your age. If you've been practicing for years, that's great—you have experience. What young people can do with hustle, you can compensate for with wisdom and knowledge. All you need is a framework, a map of sorts, and my hope is that this map I have put together can help you.

My early days working with patients who were entrepreneurs and helping clinicians who knew nothing about entrepreneurship led me to amassing a vast amount of knowledge about the business of clinician entrepreneurism that has allowed me to transform the way we think about medicine. We have this trillion-dollar industry built around sick care and treating illness. Yet, as practitioners, we are dropped off at the front gates of this system and expected to build health for the masses. We cannot—and should not be expected to—accomplish this task within a system that focusses on fixes and fails to promote health.

My intention for this book is to provide you with a roadmap for building optimal health through your chosen model of practice. IMPACT Medicine is a series of steps that you can use to successfully navigate your way through this vast frontier that has been opened before you. You can do it with Intention, Mindset, People, Attraction, Cents and Sense, and by Thinking Like an Entrepreneur.

Intention. Be clear in what you want in your practice and what you want in your own life. If you would like to have your cake and eat it too, you can. But if you don't know what you want, I can make no promises about what you are going to get.

Mindset. What are the steps that you need to have in place so that you can reach a point of confidence? How do you go to the edge of that diving board and decide that you are willing to jump in?

People. How do you actually start to build transformation for the people that you are serving? You were never taught these things in school, but you need to come up with a transformational process. The Quadrants of Care described in this book will help you formulate that process.

Attraction. You've created this transformational process that can help people, but how do you drive them to it? How do you bring people in the door? How do you get them as excited as you are about this new idea? It's all new to them, and they haven't had the privilege of seeing what it can do. A product or service without a marketing strategy is not a business. Attraction and the IMPACT Marketing System is the strategy you need to reach more people.

Cents and Sense. It's all well and good to create this transformational approach for your patients, but what if you could start to build your own income, your own wealth, and your own legacy alongside it? What if you could start doing all of these things today, not decades from now? You can't build a system for incredible, inconceivable impact yet not have a system to manage your money. Money fuels your impact. When good people make good money, they can do good things.

Think Like an Entrepreneur. You are an entrepreneur, and it's important to practice thinking that way. Think of your business as that blank canvas—you can create whatever painting you'd like. Thinking like an entrepreneur is what distinguishes art from a puddle of paint.

All you need to do now is get started. Take that single step. Put one foot in front of the other. Create something amazing for yourself and your patients. If people have health, they can change the world. You can give them that gift.

That is your first step.

If you're looking for like-minded people who are also on this journey, I invite you to head to my website at impactmedicinebook.com/resources. There, you'll find more resources and more people committed to changing the way they deliver health. Like me, they are on a mission. They are part of the mission to put our medicine in the hands of millions, and there is room for you too. Become part of the movement.

ACKNOWLEDGEMENT AND GRATITUDE

Writing a book is harder than I thought it would be. It has taken nothing short of a miracle and a community of supporters to enable the creation of IMPACT Medicine.

To my home crew, Nyah, Raelen and Bayla, you inspire me to do my best work while finding time and reason to play. Thank you for bringing balance to my life and endless inspiration to my work in the world. Greg, I could not do what I do without you. You are a partner in the truest sense of the word, and you inspire me to play bigger than I ever thought imaginable. I love you.

Mom, you are my forever-cheerleader and the inspiration for my unrelenting desire to teach and speak with unwavering conviction. Thank you for your endless support. Dad, you are the dean of my personal business education and an endless source of wisdom, guidance and inspiration. I would not be who I am without you.

To my OG business partner and friend, Erin Wiley, thank you for your unwavering love and belief in my journey and vision. Heather Allen, you are a gift with wisdom and capacity beyond words. IMPACT would not be possible or this much fun without you. Hayley Davis and the rest of the CBL team, your support means the world to me. Thank you from the bottom of my heart.

Showing up and playing outside your comfort zone is where you find those equally committed to impact and your success. Thank you to the cheerleaders and supporters who have inspired me along the way—from the classroom to the entrepreneurial circus ring— it has all played a role. Thank you for those who have advocated loud and softly: J. J. Virgin, Daniel Samson, James Maskell, Michelle Peris, Jordan Robertson, Mehran Tabrizi, Alison Danby, Susie and Neil Blair, Lauren Phelan, Janice Meredith, Mark Wade, Greg Eckel, Cassie Bjork, Jen Oliver, Bob Bernhardt, Frank Phelan, Marnie Walker, Adele Tevlin, Debbie Smrz, Andréa Proulx, Emila Brittain, Julie Durnan, Susan Hobson, Colleen McGoey, Colette Villamizar, Elan Zusman, Sheila Weitzman and so many other thoughtful and encouraging souls. Thank you from the bottom of my heart.

To Susan Paul, Mikey Kershisnik and the entire team at Lionsgate, thank you for your support, skill and spellcheck extraordinaire.

To my friends who have cheered me on, my colleagues who have taken a chance and the patients who provided confidence in my care—thank you for trying on my vision and for trusting me as a custodian and advocate of your future.

My heart is full. Thank you all.

ABOUT THE AUTHOR

DR. MEGHAN WALKER, ND INACTIVE, HBSC, is an Entrepologist (On-tre-pol-uh-gist), investor and former Naturopathic Doctor who has spent nearly two decades studying and practicing Naturopathic Medicine. As an entrepreneur, Meghan started and sold her first business while in university and has gone on to found more than five subsequent businesses and clinics in the health and wellness sector. Meghan is the host of the Impact Podcast, Founder of Entrepology Labs, Co-founder of Health Hives and Chief Cheerleader/CEO of Clinician Business Labs—a platform to assist clinicians scale and amplify their businesses.

For almost ten years, Meghan has been working with regulated practitioners from around the world to help them build scalable practices, increase their financial literacy and stay in-love with their work.

Meghan is an award-winning speaker, having spoken on international stages and through multiple media outlets on topics related to women's performance medicine, brain health and entrepreneurship. She is the host and producer of the annual entrepreneurship conference Impact LIVEs and most importantly, the bedtime story reader to her three young girls. Meghan lives in Toronto Canada with her husband and three daughters, Nyah, Raelen and Bayla.

meghanwalker.com

Instagram: @drmeghanwalker

Twitter: @drmeghanwalker

TikTok: @drmeghanwalker

INDEX

Page numbers in *italics* refer to figures.

Printed in the USA
CPSIA information can be obtained
at www.ICGtesting.com
CBHW021958280624
10733CB00003B/16